The Organisation of the Anthropocene

International Legal Theory and Practice

Volumes published in this Brill Research Perspectives title are listed at *brill.com/rplt*

The Organisation of the Anthropocene

In Our Hands?

By

Jorge E. Viñuales

BRILL

LEIDEN | BOSTON

Originally published as Volume 1.1 (2018), in *International Legal Theory and Practice*,
DOI 10.1163/24522058-01010001.

The Library of Congress Cataloging-in-Publication Data is available online at http://catalog.loc.gov
LC record available at http://lccn.loc.gov/2018946355

Typeface for the Latin, Greek, and Cyrillic scripts: "Brill". See and download: brill.com/brill-typeface.

ISBN 978-90-04-38135-3 (paperback)
ISBN 978-90-04-38136-0 (e-book)

This book is printed on acid-free paper and produced in a sustainable manner.

Contents

The Organisation of the Anthropocene

In Our Hands?

Jorge E. Viñuales
Harold Samuel Professor of Law and Environmental Policy University of Cambridge*
jev32@cam.ac.uk

Abstract

This essay introduces the legal dimensions of the Anthropocene, i.e. the currently advocated new geological epoch in which humans are the defining force. It explores in this context two basic propositions. First, law as a technology of social organisation has been neglected in the otherwise highly technology-focused accounts by natural and social scientists of the drivers of the Anthropocene. Secondly, in those rare instances where law has been discussed, there is a tendency to assume that the role of law is to tackle the negative externalities of transactions (e.g. their environmental or social implications) rather than the core of the underlying transactions, i.e. the organization of production and consumption processes. Such focus on externalities fails to unveil the role of law in prompting, sustaining and potentially managing the processes that have led to the Anthropocene. After a brief introduction to the Anthropocene narrative and the possible role of law in it, it focuses on three main questions: the disconnection between natural and human history, the profound inequalities within the human variable driving the Anthropocene, and the technological transition required to reach a sustainable societal organisation.

Keywords

Anthropocene – ontological dualism – climate change – planetary boundaries – energy transitions – inequality – human agency – environmental law – environmental externalities – law as a technology – positivism – future generations

* Harold Samuel Professor of Law and Environmental Policy, University of Cambridge, and Founder of the Cambridge Centre for Environment, Energy and Natural Resource Governance (C-EENRG). The author gratefully acknowledges the financial support of the Cambridge-PSL Fund (project 'Law in the Anthropocene' jointly with the College de France).

 | DOI 10.1163/9789004381360_002

Introduction

> Tout ce qui est avouable est comme destitué de tout avenir
> Paul Valéry, *Notes sur la grandeur et la décadence de l'Europe* (1927)

To a reader's eyes, the drafting of 'research agendas' may leave the impression of a lazy exercise. After all, an agenda is at best a pure starting-point, with no apparent research actually conducted and no conclusions reached. From a drafter's perspective, the experience of developing a research agenda or, more accurately, of framing a research problem can be a frustrating one. The considerable amount of work done upstream may not be fully reflected in the two modest results the exercise can hope to reach, namely (a) the identification of relevant research questions (including (i) not just potentially interesting questions, but foundational ones capable of federating other more specific questions, and (ii) for which legal analysis is particularly appropriate), and (b) the development of an overall analytical framework (capable (i) of organising the different questions into a meaningful order and (ii) of linking such questions to problems arising in broader and integrative natural/social science research agendas).

This essay aims to provide a research agenda to understand the role of law, broadly understood as a social and cultural practice reflected in institutions and texts, in prompting, sustaining and potentially managing the Anthropocene, the proposed new epoch of the Earth system (Geological Time Scale) where humans are the defining geological force. More fundamentally, the essay aims to frame the vast inquiry on the role of law in the Anthropocene that we, as lawyers, will face in the XXI century and explain why such an inquiry must go far beyond the narrow confines of environmental law and encompass the entirety of law and legal processes, with particular emphasis on some areas where law seems to have favoured and sustained the advent of the Anthropocene. My goal is to advance and explore two basic propositions. First, law as a technology of social organisation has been neglected in the otherwise highly technology-focused accounts by natural and social scientists of the drivers of the Anthropocene. Secondly, in those rare instances where law has been discussed in these and other accounts, there is a tendency to assume that the role of law is to tackle the negative externalities of transactions (e.g. their environmental or social implications) rather than the core of the underlying transactions (i.e. the organisation of production and consumption processes). Such focus on externalities fails, in my view, to unveil the role of law in prompting, sustaining and potentially managing the processes that have led to the Anthropocene.

It is indeed impossible to account for the development of the forces leading to the Anthropocene without a sufficient understanding of the legal dimensions at play, including the role of sovereignty (without which climate mitigation would not have presented a collective action problem), the emergence of the corporate form (which has made possible a sufficient accumulation of capital), the extension of property rights (encompassing, among others, rights over intellectual creations, such as technology), the organisation of labour relations (which has varied extensively from slavery and forced-labour to the labour rights recognised today) or that of international trade (from closed imperial systems to highly liberalised exchanges), among many others. I specifically selected these areas as examples in order to emphasise how partial a focus on laws addressing negative externalities (whether social or environmental) would be. Accepting or, more accurately, uncritically or deliberately assuming that law's role is merely to address the impact of certain transactions on third parties or on the natural environment amounts to assuming – uncritically or deliberately – that the very transactions causing these effects are desirable and should be allowed to continue. That may or may not be the case at a specific level, but it should result from a conscious, informed and legitimate decision. This is because there are legal means that could address not just the externality but the very nature of the transaction (e.g. banning slavery or certain industrial practices) or to prompt a transition away from certain transactions (e.g. phasing out certain chemicals or incentivising certain forms of energy production).

The two propositions formulated above are the conceptual thread that underpins the exploratory analysis conducted in this essay of what I see as the three main areas of inquiry that we, as lawyers and more broadly as intellectuals, should engage with to clarify the role of law in the Anthropocene. My exploration of each area is mostly intended to suggest a research agenda where legal analysis is integrated within the wider research agenda that the Anthropocene narrative, i.e. the emerging discourse about the Anthropocene as a new epoch, opens to humanities, social and natural sciences. After recalling the origins and implications of the Anthropocene narrative and elaborating on the role that law plays in it (part 1), I identify three clusters of foundational legal questions raised by this narrative, each arising from broader areas of inquiry in the humanities, social and natural sciences: the disconnection between human and natural history (part 2); the profound inequalities implied in the concept of Anthropocene (part 3); and the trade-offs entailed by sustainability transitions (part 4). The final section provides a concise statement of the research agenda proposed in this essay (A research agenda), followed by a select bibliography.

Part 1: Law in the Anthropocene Narrative

The advent of the Anthropocene is not a mere topic among others. It does stand apart for at least two reasons.

First, despite its many interpretations and uses, the term 'Anthropocene' has a common core, namely that humans have become an Earth-shaping force of geological proportions or, more specifically, that they have caused a lasting change in the Earth system.[1] The 'markers' of the Anthropocene are of

---

1 The introduction of the concept of Anthropocene in its present understanding was initially made in P. J. Crutzen, E. Stoermer, 'The « Anthropocene »' (2000) 41 *IGBP Global Change Newsletter* 17, and then more assertively in P. J. Crutzen, 'Geology of Mankind' (2002) 415 *Nature* 23. The argument was generalised in a number of publications, particularly W. Steffen, P. J. Crutzen, J. R. McNeil, 'The Anthropocene: Are humans now overwhelming the great forces of nature?' (2007) 36/8 *Ambio* 614 (expressing the narrative of the Anthropocene since its origins in the 1800s, to the 'Great Acceleration' after 1945, to nowadays, using as marker the concentration of carbon dioxide in the troposphere); W. Steffen, J. Grinevald, P. J. Crutzen, J. R. McNeill, 'The Anthropocene: Conceptual and historical perspectives' (2011) 369/1938 *Philosophical Transactions of the Royal Society* 842 (making a more general statement of the Anthropocene narrative and arguing that it must be recognised stratigraphically as the new geological era in which we live since 1800, replacing the Holocene). It has been extended in a number of ways, e.g. through the definition of planetary boundaries or by the contribution of other disciplines to identify markers: J. Rockstrom et al., 'A safe operating space for humanity' (2009) 461 *Nature* 472 (a more action oriented assessment introducing the idea of planetary boundaries – Earth's biophysical thresholds – within which human action must remain and arguing that three – carbon dioxide atmospheric concentrations, biodiversity loss, nitrogen releases – out of nine such boundaries have already been crossed); L. Robin, W. Steffen, 'History for the Anthropocene' (2007) 5/5 *History Compass* 1694 (exploring the implications of the concept of Anthropocene for the writing of integrated 'world' and 'environmental' historiography); E. C. Ellis, 'Anthropogenic transformation of the terrestrial biosphere' (2011) 369/1938 *Philosophical Transactions of the Royal Society* 1010 (arguing that only in the last century has the human transformation of the terrestrial biosphere in to anthropogenic biomes become sufficient to leave an irreversible and unambiguous geological record). There has been significant debate as to when should the Anthropocene be considered to have started: S. L. Lewis, M. A. Maslin, 'Defining the Anthropocene' (2015) 519 *Nature* 171; J. Zalasiewicz et al., 'When did the Anthropocene begin? A mid-twentieth century boundary level is stratigraphically optimal' (2015) 383 *Quaternary international* 196; Colin N. Waters et al. 'The Anthropocene is functionally and stratigraphically distinct from the Holocene' (2016) 351/6269 *Science* aad2622–1. One important critique of the Anthropocene narrative concerns the role of inequality: A. Malm, A. Hornborg, 'The geology of mankind? A critique of the Anthropocene narrative' (2014) 1/1 *The Anthropocene Review* 62 (arguing that using the human species as an analytical category in the Anthropocene narrative obscures the fact that the fossil economy was not created nor is it upheld by humankind in general, but only by part of it. Inequalities must therefore be integrated in our understanding of the ecological

different natures. In addition to the concentration of greenhouse gases in the troposphere causing climatic change,[2] the appalling rate of biodiversity loss,[3] the level of ocean acidification,[4] the radical alteration of the nitrogen[5] and phosphorous cycles[6] with the resulting eutrophication and hypoxia (asphyxiation) for aquatic life,[7] and other geochemical markers,[8] the Anthropocene can be read through 'human markers'.

The latter expression is complex. It is meant to go beyond the geophysical and geochemical markers left by humans on the Earth system and capture

---

crisis). There is now a significant body of literature on the Anthropocene. In addition to two specific journals (*Anthropocene* and *The Anthropocene Review*), several books have been published, including: C. Lorius, L. Carpentier, *Voyage dans l'Anthropocène: cette nouvelle ère dont nous sommes les héros* (Arles: Actes Sud, 2010); B. Glaser, G. Krause, B. M. W. Ratter, M. Welp (eds.), *Human-Nature Interactions in the Anthropocene* (London: Routledge, 2012); M. Whitehead, *Environmental Transformations: A Geography of the Anthropocene* (New York: Routledge, 2014); C. Hamilton, F. Gemenne, C. Bonneil (eds.), *The Anthropocene and the Global Environmental Crisis: Rethinking Modernity in a New Epoch* (London: Routledge, 2015). For two recent overviews of the literature see E. Brondizio et al.., 'Re-conceptualizing the Anthropocene: A call for collaboration' (2016) *Global Environmental Change*, advance version: http://dx.doi.org/10.1016/j.gloenvcha.2016.02.006; and the illuminating book-length study of C. Bonneuil, J.-B. Fressoz, *L'événement Anthropocène. La Terre, l'histoire et nous* (Paris: Seuil, 2016).

2 Steffen, Crutzen, McNeil (2007), above n. 1.

3 See Rockstrom et al. (2009), above n. 1; S. L. Pimm et al., 'The biodiversity of species and their rates of extinction, distribution, and protection' (2014) 344/6187 *Science* 987 (arguing that current rates of extinction are about 1000 times the likely background rate of extinction).

4 See S. Barker, A. Ridgwell, 'Ocean Acidification' (2012) 3/10 *Nature Education Knowledge* 21 (explaining ocean acidification and human impact on it); J. C. Orr et al., 'Anthropogenic ocean acidification over the twenty-first century and its impact on calcifying organisms' (2005) 437 *Nature* 681 (explaining trends in emissions and their consequences for ocean pH and certain marine organisms).

5 See Rockstrom et al. (2009), above n. 1; J. N. Galloway et al., 'Transformation of the nitrogen cycle: recent trends, questions, and potential solutions' (2008) 320/5879 *Science* 889 (describing human alterations of the nitrogen cycle as a result of combustion of fossil fuels and demand for nitrogen in agriculture and industry. Noting also nitrogen deficiencies in food-production in some parts of the world).

6 See Rockstrom et al. (2009), above n. 1; E. M. Bennet, S. R. Carpenter, N. F. Caraco, 'Human Impact on Erodable Phosphorus and Eutrophication: A Global Perspective' (2001) 51/3 *BioScience* 227 (offering an estimation of the increase in net phosphorous storage in terrestrial and freshwater ecosystems which is 75% higher than in pre-industrial times).

7 See R. J. Diaz, R. Rosenberg, 'Spreading dead zones and consequences for marine ecosystems' (2008) 321/5891 *Science* 926 (charting the expansion of 'dead zones' due to eutrophication and the resulting hypoxia).

8 See Waters et al. (2016), above n. 1 (reviewing evidence for a variety of geochemical signatures of human action or 'technofossils').

two other – subtler – types of markers, namely the impact of human activities on the characteristics of the human species (itself a part of the Earth system or, in other terms, of the biosphere) and the consolidated human practices that have enabled the other markers to emerge and spread. Some examples of the first type of human markers include changes in the chemical composition of human bodies[9] or the total amount and global distribution of human biomass.[10] Some examples of the second type of human markers include the consolidated social practices that are usually referred to with the terms 'technology' (e.g. energy production and transportation based on fossil fuels, agricultural production based on agrochemicals, warfare equipment and technology), 'institutions' (e.g. forms of social organisation, capitalistic production and exchange processes, urbanisation, legal systems) or 'culture' (e.g. consumerism, certain religious and cultural views of the world). Such social practices share the underlying trait that they have enabled (i.e. they have likely played a role, although not necessarily a causal role) humans to turn into a geological force. Understanding these consolidated social practices as human markers makes law, whether it is considered as a technology, an institution, a form of culture, a combination of these things or another consolidated social practice, a possible human marker of the Anthropocene, alongside the other markers.

Unsurprisingly, whereas the existence of a link between, on the one hand, these human activities combined and, on the other hand, the profound impacts on the Earth system is less and less controversial, the specific interrelations between different phenomena are becoming more and more so. To give a sense of how much the debate is shifting towards the controversial specificities, it will suffice to recall some of the main questions asked: is the overexploitation of resources that characterises the Anthropocene a result of

9 See D. Smith, 'Worldwide trends in DDT levels in human breast milk' (1999) 28 *International Journal of Epidemiology* 179 (tracking contamination of human breast milk by the persistent organic pollutant DDT); QQ Li et al., 'Persistent organic pollutants and adverse health effects in humans' (2006) 69/21 *Journal of Toxicology and Environmental Health/A* 1987 (review article on the state of knowledge on residual levels of persistent organic pollutant concentrations in human adipose tissue worldwide, before moving to the case of Singapore).

10 See S. Walpole et al., 'The weight of nations: An estimation of adult human biomass' (2012) 12/439 *BMC Public Health*, available at http://www.biomedcentral.com/1471-2458/12/439 (according to whom, in 2005, global adult human biomass was approximately 287 million tonnes, of which 15 million tonnes were due to overweight, a mass equivalent to that of 242 million people of average body mass. North America has 6% of the world population but 34% of biomass due to obesity. Asia has 61% of the world population but 13% of biomass).

capitalism? Who has benefitted and who has not? Is there a debt towards the latter or towards future generations? Has the unprecedented development of military capacity led to the Anthropocene? Has science, with the opening of new frontiers and possibilities, resulted in the Anthropocene? Have religious beliefs – placing humans as 'masters' of the 'creation' – or cultural beliefs – modernity and 'progress' – led to the Anthropocene? None of these questions can be fully and definitively answered, but each one can be illuminated to an extent sufficient to enable understanding and perhaps meaningful change in the relevant human facts.

This leads me to the second reason why the Anthropocene is not a mere topic among others, namely that the advent of the Anthropocene raises all these questions at once. It calls upon all disciplines, the entire body of human knowledge about the world, to analyse what is happening and how to face it. As noted in a 2016 review article covering a good part of the emerging literature on the Anthropocene '[f]ew global change science concepts have enjoyed such a broad and rapid uptake in technical and public discourses despite a long history of scholarship exploring human interactions with the global environment'.[11] This is true of natural sciences but also of social sciences and humanities.[12] However, it is not true of law and lawyers, not yet. The above review article does not even mention legal disciplines as part of the integrative approach, and legal aspects are also neglected or, at best, only mentioned in passing in other major efforts to extend the conversation beyond natural sciences.[13] This is not surprising because law and legal studies have been considered – and institutionally organised – as a separate subject for centuries. Lawyers are partly responsible. We spend far too much time speaking to each other, and our conceptions of interdisciplinarity have remained fairly simplistic.

In the last few years, however, the Anthropocene theme has started, albeit timidly, to permeate legal studies. So far, there have been three main sets of

11 Brondizio et al. (2016), above n. 1, at 2.

12 See G. Palsson et al., 'Reconceptualizing the 'Anthropos' in the Anthropocene: integrating the social sciences and humanities in global environmental change research' (2013) 28 *Environmental Science and Policy* 1 (overlooking law in its attempt to integrate social sciences and humanities); N. Castree et al., 'Changing the intellectual climate' (2014) 4 *Nature Climate Change* 763 (mentioning, as part of the 'missing human dimensions', the need to integrate environmental lawyers, but without any further development).

13 See Palsson et al. (2013), above n. 12; Castree et al. (2014), above n. 12; N. Castree, 'The Anthropocene and the Environmental Humanities: Extending the Conversation' (2014) 5 *Environmental Humanities* 233 (mentioning environmental lawyers as those to whom the conversation should be extended, but without any further discussion).

contributions from lawyers to the role of law in the Anthropocene, including two books,[14] one issue of a major legal journal,[15] and a small number of articles.[16] The great majority come from environmental lawyers, and they have

14 See A. S. Garmestani, C. R. Allen (eds.), *Social–Ecological Resilience and Law* (New York: Columbia University Press, 2014) (focusing on the need for adaptive law-making to face the challenges of the Anthropocene); L. Kotzè, *Global Environmental Constitutionalism in the Anthropocene* (Oxford: Hart Publishing, 2016) (arguing for a reconceptualization of environmental constitutionalism to face the challenges of the Anthropocene and for its generalisation at the international level).

15 See *Yearbook of International Environmental Law* (2014) 25 (1) (including four articles specifically focusing on the Anthropocene concept and its relevance for international law – Vidas, Zalasiewicz, Williams –, its constitutional potential – Kotzè –, the role of ecological integrity within international environmental law – Bridgewater, Kim, Bosselmann –, and the impact of the Anthropocene concept on the doctrine on international environmental law – Vordermayer).

16 The authors of these articles are recurrent and their different contributions tend to expand on their earlier arguments. See e.g. Nicholas Robinson: 'Beyond Sustainability: Environmental Management for the Anthropocene Epoch' (2012) 12 *Journal of Public Affairs* 181 (arguing that sustainable development is insufficient to rise to the challenges of the Anthropocene and that resort to two fundamental principles, cooperation and resilience, is necessary); 'Fundamental Principles of Law for the Anthropocene?' (2014) 44 *Environmental Policy and Law* 1 (identifying ways of legally enhancing the concept of sustainability – through environmental rights and several principles such as cooperation, nature stewardship, resilience, foresight, sufficiency, well-being, and justice – in order to manage the environmental challenges of the Anthropocene); Eric Biber, 'Law in the Anthropocene Epoch' (2016) *UC Berkeley Public Law Research Paper No. 2834037* (2 September 2016) (exploring the implications of the stress placed by the Anthropocene on certain concepts of private and public American law); Louis Kotzé: 'Rethinking Global Environmental Law and Governance in the Anthropocene' (2014) 32 *Journal of Energy and Natural Resources Law* 121 (attempting to mainstream the Anthropocene concept within environmental law discourse); 'Human Rights and the Environment in the Anthropocene' (2014) 1 *The Anthropocene Review* 1 (arguing that the role of human rights in connection with environmental protection must be fundamentally redefined to take into account the Anthropocene); Klaus Bosselmann: K. Rakhyun and K. Bosselmann, 'International Environmental Law in the Anthropocene: Towards a Purposive System of Multilateral Environmental Agreements' (2013) 2 *Transnational Environmental Law* 285 (arguing that in order for multilateral environmental agreements to become effective they should all be considered to target a single goal, namely the integrity of Earth's life-support system. This idea is further developed in a subsequent co-authored article in the Yearbook of International Environmental Law); Davor Vidas: D. Vidas, O. K. Fauchald, Ø. Jensen, M. W. Tvedt, 'International law for the Anthropocene? Shifting perspectives in regulation of the oceans, environment and genetic resources' (2015) 9 *Anthropocene* 1 (discussing the implications of the Anthropocene for two assumptions underpinning international law, namely the quest for stability in international relations and the assumption of stability in the natural substrate). Professor Vidas has been very active in integrating the Anthropocene concept into international legal scholarship, and he has participated in a variety of non-legal publications as well. Finally, two other articles use the term

mostly appeared in environmentally-minded platforms. This is understandable but problematic. Environmental law, whether at the domestic or at the international level, has been built upon the idea that its purpose and *raison d'être* is to tackle the adverse effects of transactions on those who do not take part in them, whether third parties or the environment (negative externalities). The initial Pigouvian idea of correcting this market dysfunction through policy intervention (a tax),[17] further developed by R. Coase in the 1960s (with a focus on trading),[18] was already at play in the early 1800s, roughly a century before its formal conceptualisation in economic theory. The early examples of environmental laws concerned the nuisance arising from industrial activities and their target, as I shall discuss later, was not to block the activity but to address the effects through compensation or the application of a regulatory system (involving authorisation, relocation and inspection). Despite the great sophistication of contemporary environmental law systems,[19] there has been little change in its overall focus. This is particularly so with the increasing influence of market-based approaches to environmental protection,[20] which emphasise the internalisation of negative externalities, even for externalities that exceed the threshold of significant or even serious damage.[21] What better example of a monstrous 'externality' than the Anthropocene itself? We need to go beyond addressing externalities and concentrate on addressing the transactions themselves. In other words, we need to go beyond 'environmental' law, in its present understanding as the law tackling negative externalities, and focus on how

Anthropocene but, in fairness, it is more accurate to place them among the literature on climate change law: K. N. Scott, 'International law in the Anthropocene: Responding to the Geoengineering Challenge' (2012) 34 *Michigan Journal of International Law* 309 (referring to the Anthropocene as the background of geoengineering but only identifying some well-known principles of international environmental law as applicable to the governance of geoengineering); S. H. Baker, 'Adaptive Law in the Anthropocene' (2015) 90 *Chicago-Kent Law Review* 563 (focusing on the inadequacy of current strategies to adaptation to climate change and arguing for adaptive legal principles).

17 See A. C. Pigou, *The Economics of Welfare* (London: Mcmillan, 1920).

18 See R. Coase, 'The Problem of Social Cost' (1960) 3 *Journal of Law and Economics* 1.

19 On domestic environmental law systems see E. Lees, J. E. Vinuales (eds), *The Oxford Handbook of Comparative Environmental Law* (Oxford University Press, forthcoming 2018). On international environmental law see P.-M. Dupuy, J. E. Viñuales, *International Environmental Law* (Cambridge University Press, 2015, 2nd edn. 2018).

20 For an overview see J. Freeman, C. Kolstad (eds.), *Moving to Markets in Environmental Regulation. Lessons from Twenty Years of Experience* (Oxford University Press, 2006).

21 See J. E. Viñuales, 'La distribution de la charge de protéger l'environnement: Expressions juridiques de la solidarité', in A. Supiot (ed.), *Face à l'irresponsabilité: La dynamique de la solidarité* (Paris: Conférences du College de France, 2018), at 19–36.

law more generally organises the transactions or processes that prompted the Anthropocene.

This wider focus is by no means foreign to the Anthropocene narrative; quite to the contrary. In the founding modern narrative of the Anthropocene, P. Crutzen situates its origins in the late eighteen century and links this date to the granting, in 1784, of an intellectual property right (a patent) to the Scottish scientist James Watt on a new version (using a separate condenser) of the steam-powered engine.[22] Such a link is not merely anecdotal. The modern steam-powered engine is considered to be the basis of the 'thermo-industrial Revolution' that generalised the massive use of fossil fuels, particularly coal.[23] Nor is the role of law in this symbolic origin anecdotal. Intellectual property rights are major tools for technology development, but also for technology entrenchment. Rather than looking merely at environmental protection laws to understand the role of law in the Anthropocene, lawyers would do well to look more widely at the laws shaping industrial organisation, working conditions, trade and investment, taxation and wealth distribution, or the very organisation of Nation-State system. We should even go further and revisit fundamental legal categories, such as 'causality', 'subject', 'obligation', 'property', 'responsibility/liability', 'legal personality', 'corporation', 'constitution', 'sovereignty' to understand how they may have played (and may still play) a role in prompting and sustaining the Anthropocene as well as how they may be adjusted or perhaps replaced in the law of more resilient and more respectful human societies.

The task for lawyers and, in fact, for all those who seek to understand the implications of the Anthropocene narrative, is to look at law as one of the major technologies accounting for the Anthropocene; a 'soft' technology alongside the 'hard' technologies relating to energy, agriculture, chemicals, building, transportation, and others that seem to have captured most of the attention. It is important to understand that the way in which States or corporations or trade, investment and financial systems are organised is not of marginal importance to the emergence and operation of 'hard' technologies. An apposite illustration is provided by the conundrums of climate change mitigation policies. The existence of a collective action problem whereby the benefits of fossil fuel use are local (electricity, heat and transportation fuelling a country's economy) and the costs (in terms of emissions of carbon dioxide) are spread

---

22 Crutzen (2002), above n. 1.

23 See J. Grinevald, 'L'effet de serre et la civilisation thermo-industrielle 1896–1996' (1997) 108 *Revue européenne des sciences sociales* 141.

across the entire globe presupposes the existence of sovereign and independent States, each with their own interests and right to pursue their own policies. Another illustration is given by the influence of the Organisation of Petroleum Exporting Countries (OPEC) on the price of oil (including its actual extraction and use, investment in further capacity and potential 'lock-ins' but also the ability of other technologies to emerge and disseminate in the face of price competition), which is premised on the sovereignty of States to use their natural resources in the way they see fit. In the past, such powers have been used to punish or pressurise oil-importing countries for political reasons or to drive potential competitors out of business. Aside from these two illustrations, the organisation of the international society in the form of sovereign States has many other implications regarding trade (or protectionism), investment, financial flows but also migration, disaster response or even disarmament (or arms races). The legal concept of sovereignty and its implications for the structure of both international and domestic law are, of course, the manifestation of social and political forces constantly at play. But the reflection of such forces through specific legal arrangements has profound implications on the activities driving the Anthropocene and, when disregarded (e.g. tensions regarding entitlements of different countries over a resource-rich and strategically important area) they could lead to devastating conflict.

Understanding the complex role of law as a technology in prompting, sustaining and potentially managing the Anthropocene is a far-reaching enterprise that cannot be conducted without some meaningful order or, in other words, without an initial reflexion on what are the most salient questions that need to be addressed and how they relate to each other and to the broader set of questions addressed in other disciplines of the humanities, social and natural sciences. The purpose of the following sections is to identify three broad clusters of questions for which the role of law is, in my view, particularly relevant. These clusters of questions are selected not only because of their importance to understand the role of law and legal analysis in the Anthropocene but also because they create bridges with the wider and integrative research agendas arising from both natural sciences and environmental humanities and social sciences. As in many other disciplines of human knowledge, the Anthropocene calls for a more general and comprehensive picture of the role of law rather than for ever-narrower specialisation. I would like to state this simple point as clearly as possible from the outset: if the role of law in prompting, sustaining and potentially managing the Anthropocene is to be elucidated and understood, it will not be through a specialised focus on or even an expansion of 'environmental law'. We must instead revisit law in its entirety to understand its role in the Anthropocene. We must look at how our new condition, not merely as immersed in the Earth system but as a major driver of it, is related to law as a consolidated social practice or to some specific expressions of such practice at given points in time and space. We must look at the very DNA of law. I hope that this essay will help to clarify why.

Part 2: Ingraining Nature in Law

1 *Preliminary Observations*

It is important, in designing the contours of this research agenda, to keep a clear focus on the role of law. This observation is intended to reassure impatient lawyers (or others interested in the role of law in the Anthropocene) as to the need for the detour that I am about to make. The detour is about the understanding of human agency in something as vast as geological time, where humans are latecomers and where there is a pervasive impression that the history and behaviour of humans is as irrelevant to the evolution of the Earth system as the latter is to the understanding of the former.

There are many ways of formulating the disconnection between these two strata and I will review some of them later on, but the thrust of the disconnection or 'dualism' argument, which justifies the detour, holds (i) that human behaviour is too marginal a variable when it comes to understanding something as vast as geological evolution, (ii) that the connection between human history and environmental constraints may only be relevant in that environmental conditions affect humans, (iii) that the environmental conditions affecting humans are themselves cyclical and, with rare exceptions, such cycles remain unperturbed in a human timescale and (iv) in all events, modern technology – since the Industrial Revolution – has released human history from environmental constraints, which, given human newly acquired technological powers, are at best a variable among many others explaining human historical events as well as individual and social behaviour (a proposition underpinning several, perhaps most, social sciences and the foundations of modern philosophy since at least Descartes). In this regard, the Anthropocene concept has two main implications: first, contrary to proposition (i), human behaviour is not at all a marginal variable in geological evolution but may well be a definitional one; secondly, contrary to propositions (iii) and (iv), the potentially considerable environmental effects of human action not only on the Earth system but also – thereby – on humans themselves call for a fundamental re-examination of our knowledge of the interactions between human action and natural processes.

I will now analyse the implications of these propositions for the underpinnings of humanities and social sciences, and hence for law. I should add that the detour is not only intended to clarify the implications of the dualism debate for law but also to integrate the potential contribution of legal analysis into a broader research agenda on the Anthropocene.

2 *Human Action and the Earth System*

Many works have charted the disconnection between natural history (and geological evolution) and human history as well as its implications.[24] In an oft-cited article, the historian Dipesh Chakrabarti has taken stock of some of this work and looked more closely at the implications of human agency on climate change for the writing of history.[25] His basic proposition is that 'anthropogenic explanations of climate change spell the collapse of the age-old humanist distinction between natural history and human history'.[26] To flesh out the meaning of this point, he refers to several towering figures ranging from Giambattista Vico – or more specifically the interpretation of the latter's work by Benedetto Croce[27] – to Robin G. Collingwood to E. H. Carr,[28] whose work contributed to play down the importance of geological time for the understanding of human history. Indeed, over the XIX century the realisation of the depth and scale of geological time[29] led to the conclusion that this stratum moved so slowly that its pace was almost imperceptible to the human eye and was better treated as an external and constant stage within which human history unfolded.[30] Nature was thus seen as external and transcending human history.

---

24 See P. Rossi, *I segni del tempo: storia della Terra e storia delle nazioni da Hooke a Vico* (Milano: Feltrinelli, 1979) (providing a detailed history of the parallel evolution of natural and human historiography).

25 D. Chakrabarty, 'The climate of history: four theses' (2009) 35 *Critical Inquiry* 197.

26 *Ibid.*, at 21.

27 B. Croce, *La filosofia di Giambattista Vico* (Bari: Laterza, 2nd edn 1922), translated into English by R. G. Colingwood.

28 E. H. Carr, *What is History?* (Cambridge University Press, 1961).

29 D. Smail identifies three main intellectual contributions as the pillars of this revolution in the understanding of time, namely C. Darwin's *On the Origin of Species* (1859), C. Lyell's *The Geological Evidences of the Antiquity of Man* (1863), and J. Lubbock's *Pre-Historic Times* (1865), D. L. Smail, *On Deep History and the Brain* (Berkeley: University of California Press, 2008), at 26.

30 Bonneuil et Fressoz illustrate this point with the converging views of two eminent XIX century academics, the French historian Jules Michelet and the British geologist Charles Llyell. For Michelet 'Since the beginning of the world a war started that will only end with the end of the world, not before; the war of man against nature, of spirit against matter, of freedom against fatality. History is nothing but the narrative of this everlasting fight […] What must encourage us in this fight without end, is the fact that, overall, one of the terms

An analogous – albeit not entirely similar – disconnection lies at the foundations of social science since the XIX century. Here, the interaction targeted is that between human action and environmental constraints, and the disconnection between the two is seen as a condition for the emergence of a science of society and its dynamics.[31] In this context, the external character of natural processes and environmental constraints has a different root-cause than in historiography, namely the ability to escape environmental constraints based on the technological powers acquired by humans since the Industrial Revolution. But the end result, the disconnection of human and natural history and, more specifically, the independence of human action from natural constraints (reflected in the disciplines aimed at its understanding) is similar.

Such a disconnection can be illustrated by the way mainstream environmental economics treats human impact on the environment, which is mostly through the microeconomic prism of market failures and externalities. At the macroeconomic level, the standard dynamic stochastic general equilibrium (DSGE) model[32] has rarely been used, if at all, to account for the impact of environmental degradation, perhaps because it is intended to look at a short time horizon. This family of models could perhaps incorporate wider environmental constraints, but mostly as an external shock or exogenous disturbance

---

does not change, and the other does change and becomes stronger. Nature remains the same, whereas every day man takes some advantage over it', Jules Michelet, *Introduction à l'histoire universelle* (Paris: Hachette, 1831), at 5–7. A similar view is expressed by Lyell from the perspective of geology. He hypothesises that an 'intelligent being' observing the action of humans may at first have the impression that human agency can change nature 'but he would soon perceive that no one of the fixed and constant laws of the animate or inanimate world was subverted by human agency, and that the modifications produced were on the occurrence of new and extraordinary circumstances, and those not of a physical, but a moral nature. The deviation permitted, would also appear to be as slight as was consistent with the accomplishment of the new moral ends proposed, and to be in great degree temporary in its nature, so that whenever the power of the new agent was withheld, even for a brief period, a relapse would take place to the ancient state of things', C. Lyell, *Principles of Geology, being an Attempt to Explain the Former Changes of the Earth's Surface, by Reference to Causes Now in Operation* (London: John Murray, 1830), vol. 1, at 164. Both referred to in Bonneil/Fressoz, above n. 1, 41–42 (our translation of Michelet's French text).

31 See e.g. A. Comte, *Cours de philosophie positive* (Paris: Bachelier, 1839), vol. 4, at 251 ('The local physical causes, very powerful at the origins of civilisation, have progressively lost their grip as the natural course of human development increasingly allows to neutralise their action'), Bonneil/Fressoz, above n. 1, at 45 (our translation of the French text).

32 The origins of DSGE modelling in neoclassical economics are often situated in the paper by F. E. Kydland, E. C. Prescott, 'Time to Build and Aggregate Fluctuations' (1982) 50/6 *Econometrica* 1345.

of the normal economic processes. In other words, environmental constraints and environmental change (e.g. natural resource depletion or pollution) are not part of such 'normal' processes, not even the changes of geological scale unveiled by the Anthropocene concept. They are 'external' or abnormal or, to continue the line of reasoning introduced earlier in this essay, they are not part of core transactions. An important question in this regard concerns the extent to which the understanding of human behaviour that arises from a social science as influential as economics can continue to treat environmental change as merely external, even as a major stochastic shock, or should instead integrate it as part of its foundations or 'normality'.

In both humanities – here historiography[33] – and social sciences – here economics[34] – there have been major efforts at addressing this disconnection through the creation of new disciplines or clusters of disciplines. As I shall discuss next, the disconnection has also characterised law but, unlike other disciplines, law has until recently remained impervious to the Anthropocene's core message.

3 *The Disconnection between Law and Nature*

3.1 Overview

The perceived disconnection between the natural and the human strata also underpins our contemporary understanding of law. Much like mainstream historiography and economics, in the last two centuries, law and legal studies have increasingly treated nature as an external object.

This can be observed from three main perspectives, namely the deliberate detachment of law from nature (or the ontological dualism of the natural and human strata in law) in positivistic accounts of law (3.2.), the expanded horizon of law in the Anthropocene as a normative construct regulating the actions of the human geological force (3.3.), and the need to go beyond the mere regulation of negative externalities in order to genuinely ingrain nature in law (3.4.).

The conceptions of nature underpinning these perspectives vary. Positivistic accounts of law first attempted to disentangle law from some

33 See e.g. Robin/Steffen, above n. 1; Chakrabarty, above n. 25; E. Russell, *Evolutionary History: Uniting History and Biology to Understand Life on Earth* (Cambridge University Press, 2011).

34 A pioneer study was published in 1971 by N. Georgescu-Roegen, *The Enthropy Law and the Economic Process* (Cambridge MA: Harvard University Press, 1971). For an overview of the now well developed field of ecological economics see R. Costanza, 'What is Ecological Economics?' (1989) 1 *Ecological Economics* 1.

religious conceptions, while still relying on other metaphysical conceptions of morals. Even in the attempt at developing a 'pure' conception of law, the legal technology distilled remains tributary of certain ontological conceptions. Yet, positivism, at least in its purest forms, is largely indifferent to whether the understanding of nature refers to a created nature spanning a few thousand years or a biosphere (today we would say an Earth system) consisting of constantly interacting processes spanning billions of years. For positivism, the goal is for law to become a value-free technology. The specific conception of nature is more important from the second perspective, because it is only in some conceptions that humans may at all become a geological force whose impact must be kept under check. This is also the case from the third perspective because different conceptions of nature entail different conceptions of the relations between humans and nature, which, in turn, shape the way in which human action is modelled (as a mere externality to be corrected or as a dynamic force capable of triggering change of – rather than change within – the system).

3.2 Law Detached from Nature

3.2.1 *An (Un-)Intended Consequence of Legal Positivism*

The rise of a certain form of legal positivism can be compared, in many ways, to the process through which humanities and social sciences were detached from geological time and environmental constraints. As a philosophical matter, legal positivism, in its more condensed understanding, holds that whether a norm is law or not does not depend on its content but on how it has been created (posited).[35] There is of course much debate not only about the truth of this proposition but also about the extent to which it accurately depicts the core of legal positivism. It is, however, on a different plane that legal positivism deserves attention here, namely as an influential understanding of law and legal processes.

From the perspective of intellectual history, legal positivism can indeed be considered as a declaration of independence from religion, morals but also natural reason or other metaphysical accounts. It is an attempt at building a

35 This foundational meaning is usually traced back to the work of J. Austin, *The Province of Jurisprudence Determined* (London: John Murray, 1832). Legal positivism is traditionally understood as having emerged with the philosophical work of Jeremy Bentham (*Of Laws in General*, London: Athlone Press, 1970 [1782]), influenced by the works of David Hume and Thomas Hobbes, and influencing Austin and his conception of 'command'. Two different conceptions of legal positivism which have exercised immense influence over the XX century are those of Hans Kelsen (*Reine Rechtslehre: Einleitung in die rechtswissenschaftiche Problematik* (Leipzig; Wien: F. Deuticke, 1934)) and Herbert Hart (*The Concept of Law* (Oxford: Clarendon Press, 1961)).

true 'science of law' (*Rechtswissenschaft*) which, in the first positivist accounts, was to be independent from certain specific metaphysical conceptions of nature[36] and, in time, it aimed at not being reliant on any such conception. Such a science of law was to focus on humans and not – in any way – on nature. The dissociation of the human and natural strata is particularly visible in some expressions of legal positivism. The immensely influential work of the Austrian jurist Hans Kelsen attempted to and, in many ways, succeeded in developing law as a detached technology. I do not mean by this that the conceptual construction of Kelsen (or other supporters of legal positivism) is flawless and that it actually managed, from a theoretical standpoint, to evacuate metaphysics. It is as an intellectual and social project, as an effort to mobilise lawyers and other intellectuals into thinking about law differently, that positivism has thrived, much like empirical – particularly quantitative – approaches to social science (from sociology, to economics, to political science) have thrived since the second half of the XX century.

Detaching law and its science from metaphysical conceptions of nature was thus an enterprise comparable to that of building empirical (by contrast to normative) social sciences. As an enterprise it had, and still has great merit, and it enabled great advances in the way law is created, applied and analysed. Yet, much like for humanities and social sciences, legal positivism deliberately sought to dissociate any conception of nature from the foundations and remit of a science of law. As noted in Kelsen's preface to a synthesis volume in English (*General Theory of Law and the State*) bringing together and reorganising his work on the 'pure theory of law':

> When this doctrine is called the 'pure theory of law', it is meant that it is being kept free from all the elements foreign to the specific method of a science whose only purpose is the cognition of law, not its formation. A science has to describe its object as it actually is, not to prescribe how it should be or should not be from the point of view of some specific value judgments. The latter is a problem of politics and, as such, concerns the art of government, an activity directed at values, not an object of science, directed at reality. *The reality, however, at which a science of law is directed, is not the reality of nature which constitutes the object of natural science. If it is necessary to separate the science of law from politics, it is no*

36 See D. Priel, 'Toward Classical Legal Positivism' (2015) 101 *Virginia Law Review* 987 (arguing that, in fact, Hobbes and Bentham understood their theory of law as derived from a broader – if idionsyncratic – metaphysical conception, distinct from that of natural law proponents).

> *less necessary to separate it from natural science. One of the most difficult tasks of a general theory of law is that of determining the specific reality of its subject and of showing the difference that exists between legal and natural reality.*[37]

The representative value of this opening statement, or of a major book, or even of a major author, such as Kelsen, is of course not enough to demonstrate that law underwent a disconnection analogous to that of other disciplines. It is offered here as a carefully selected illustration of this forceful and influential attempt.

The phenomenon illustrated here by the reference to H. Kelsen's writings was charted in the early 1900s by one of the most prominent and influential social thinkers of the century, namely Max Weber.[38] Weber saw in the higher level of 'rationality' of European law, as compared to the laws of other regions, one of the explanations of the rise of industrial capitalism in the West. By rationality, Weber meant a variety of features of European law including a highly differentiated legal organisation (distinct from political administration and religion, and in the hands of a specialised professional class of lawyers), a creation process that emphasised the conscious and deliberate act of making law as detached from immutable tradition and religious interference, and concrete decision-making based on prior rules of general and universal application. Importantly, Weber clarified that capitalism was not itself the driver of the special features of European law but, rather, that such features had been particularly favourable for the emergence of industrial capitalism. What led to the development of a European law with distinct features is a type of political organisation, the bureaucratically organised State, relying not on tradition or charismatic power but increasingly on logically formal rationality. And what made rational law socially effective was a combination of factors including the historical separation in Europe of the spiritual and secular orders, the influence of Roman law, the bureaucratic organisation of the Catholic Church itself,

37 H. Kelsen, *General Theory of Law and the State* (Cambridge MA: Harvard University Press, 1945), at xiv (italics added).

38 M. Weber, *Wirtschaft und Gesellschaft. Grundriss der verstehenden Soziologie* (Tubingen: J. C. B. Mohr, 4th edn 1956). English translation: *Economy and Society. An Outline of Interpretive Sociology* (Berkeley: University of California Press, edn by G. Roth & R. Wittich, 1968), part II, section VIII: Economy and Law (The Sociology of Law), at 641ff. For an illuminating study of the link between the development of Western capitalism and the rationalisation of law in Weber's writings see D. M. Trubek, 'Max Weber on Law and the Rise of Capitalism' (1972) *Wisconsin Law Review* 720. In this paragraph, I follow Trubek's account.

the use of legally organised and trained bureaucracies for rulers to impose their power, the need to compose with social constituencies – particularly the bourgeoisie – to consolidate such power, and the functional separation of activities within the legal sphere between the enactment of law and its application to concrete situations.[39] The higher level of rationality that Weber ascribed to European law can be equated, although he did not frame the question in those terms,[40] to the more positivistic or technical nature of such law. This is particularly clear as regards the functional specialisation of law and law-making processes. And a system of rational and generally applicable law is particularly favourable to the development of capitalism because of its higher predictability (calculability or what we would today call 'optimisation') and, substantively, the room it would allow for market freedoms and contractual practices.[41] The latter point highlights the interest of rational positivistic law as a form of market organisation law but it also suggests that market forces were supposed to be left evolve according to their own interests. As summarised by D. M. Trubek:

> At least some areas of social life had to be freed of the bonds of kinship, religion, and other foci of traditional authority, and, at the same time, insulated from the arbitrary action of the state. This required that the state, as legal order, be strengthened, so that it superseded other sources of social control, and at the same time be limited, so that it did not encroach upon areas of economic action. The state was to provide a formal order, or facilitative framework within which free economic actors could operate.[42]

This is precisely the conception according to which first comes the ability to transact and only then the consideration and potential regulation of its effects on third parties (e.g. neighbours or workers) or the environment.

In stating this conclusion, it is not my intention to take a stance on the merits of legal positivism (or the conception of law as a technology) as compared to the – often simplified[43] – natural law conceptions against which positivism

---

39 See Trubek, above n. 38, at 738.

40 In fact, Weber took into account the wide acceptance in the Western world of the idea of a rational natural law that would provide further support for the rational and general rules governing the State. See *ibid*, at 738.

41 *Ibid*, at 740.

42 *Ibid*, at 744.

43 The 'natural law' against which positivism reacted was a stylised conception hardly representative of the complexity and variety of a historical tradition dating back to at least

reacted. Both may have desirable and undesirable implications. Understanding law only as technology detaches it from any underpinning values and makes it capable of serving the most reprehensible aims, as has been widely shown by the laws of Nazi Germany or South Africa under the apartheid regime. It may be argued, however, that these and other infamous misuses of a legal order are, in fact, expressions of 'naturalised' law in that law is used to translate a purported 'natural order', whether it is Aryan or White supremacy. But the distinction can be made in a less extreme context, which will perhaps be more telling. Asked about the meaning for a farmer in Ancient Greece of the unrelenting labouring of his land, the French Hellenist J.-P. Vernent answered that it should be seen as a prayer, an act through which the farmer participated in the order of the World.[44] How different this is from the work on an assembly line or even in a farm when purpose is lost. As often noted by Alain Supiot, when labour is organised in a commoditised manner, the very purpose of work becomes, at best, a secondary matter. In an analogous manner, two different conceptions of law, one as an expression of the natural order with a transcending purpose or the other as an optimisation technology with a focus on efficiency, may lead to very different conceptions of the meaning of work. But (re-)naturalising law may be far from a panacea as well, as suggested by the diminished status of the Dalit in India who, despite many governmental attempts – including a Constitutional clause – to improve their condition, are still viewed and largely treated as beyond the natural order of Hinduism. The same would be true of any oppressive legal organisation that claims to be based on a natural order or natural selection. The point I hope to make is therefore much simpler and of an empirical character. Disconnecting law from its embeddedness in religious, moral and cultural values has implications for the development of law as a discipline and a social process. As discussed next, such implications transpire in the very ontology reflected in a given legal order.

3.2.2 *Illustration: Conceptions of Property*

An example can help illustrate how different conceptions of nature translate into different legal ontologies and how deliberately displacing any relation to such conceptions (and implicitly endorsing some others) is not an innocuous step.

The idea of property can be translated into many different legal forms, each with different implications. The way in which property is organised in a given

Ancient Greece and perhaps earlier.

44 I am indebted to Alain Supiot for sharing with me his conversation with Jean-Pierre Vernent on this topic.

legal order reflects normative conceptions of the world or, in most cases, sedimented layers of such conceptions. Thus, whereas there may be significant overlaps between the conceptions of property in civil law systems (as the 'sum of its attributes') and the Anglo-American doctrine of property as a 'bundle of rights',[45] the two ontologies differ at the very least in their representation of the powers and duties of the property holder. The Roman-influenced top-down characterisation found in most civil law systems (property as a sum of three pre-defined conceptual attributes, i.e. *usus, fructus* and *abusus*[46]) is less case-specific and fine-grained that the variety of rights, prerogatives and duties – more than eleven according to some authors[47] – that together characterise property (or ownership) in bottom-up common law systems (which appear mostly as collections of observations more or less generalised into a set of categories). In turn, none of these conceptions, however detailed, pay genuine attention to potential harm to future generations or the environment as such. At best, they capture it tangentially or through significant conceptual re-elaboration.[48] For these other dimensions to be brought into the picture, resort to other related concepts such as the public trust doctrine[49] or the principle of inter-generational equity[50] or, still, some regulatory duties to protect land, wildlife, forests or waterbodies, appear necessary. In the classical conceptions of property, either in the civil or common law traditions, negative externalities were only taken into account or even identified to a limited extent, mostly in the form of civil responsibility or tort law or of some good neighbourliness duties. Concepts such as the public trust doctrine or inter-generational equity or, more generally, regulatory duties concerning the environment were

45 Y. Emerich, 'Regard civiliste sur le droit des biens de la common law: pour une conception transsystémique de la propriété' (2008) 38 *Revue générale de droit* 339, at 346–349.

46 *Ibid.*, at 346, referring to the foundational work of C. Aubry, C.-F. Rau, *Cours de droit civil français* (Paris: Librairies techniques, 7nd edn by P. Esmein, 1961), vol. 2, at 236–238.

47 *Ibid.*, at 347, referring to A. M. Honoré, 'Ownership', in A. G. Guest (ed.), *Oxford Essays in Jurisprudence* (Oxford University Press, 1961), at 107–147, at 113.

48 See e.g. the doctrine of the 'ecological function of property' developed by the High Court of Brazil (Supremo Tribunal de Justiça) in See S.T.J., REsp No. 1.240.122/PR, at 7–9, 2d Panel, Rel. Min. Antonio Herman Benjamin, 28.06.2009, D.Je. 11.09.2012.

49 See J. L. Sax, 'The Public Trust Doctrine in Natural Resources Law: Effective Judicial Intervention' (1970) 68 *Michigan Law Review* 471. For a practical application, see the decision of the Supreme Court of India in *Mehta v. Kamal Nath* et al. (1996), [1997] 1 SSC 388.

50 See E. Brown Weiss, 'The Planetary Trust: Conservation and Intergenerational Equity', (1984) 11 *Ecology Law Quarterly* 495. For a practical application see the decision of the Supreme Court of the Philippines in *Minors Oposa v Secretary of the Department of Environment and Natural Resources* (DENR) 33 ILM (1994) 173 (30 July 1993).

borrowed from other contexts or simply added as a layer of law placing bounds on the enjoyment of property.

The need for resorting to such other external or additional concepts to capture externalities contrasts sharply with the conception of communal property of some indigenous peoples, where land is never fully held by an individual but belongs to the community – past, present and future – as a whole. In such conceptions, respect for future generations and land itself is deeply ingrained in the very idea that such communities have of what we call property and does not require an additional layer of duties. The level at which this difference can be situated is not limited to the concept of property but concerns the entire legal ontology ingrained in the community's conception of law. Legal or normative notions can seldom be described in isolation because their very characterisation relies on their relations to other such notions. The practical consequences of such a distinction for the legal organisation of human relations to nature must not be underestimated, and they have been recognised in practice in several cases concerning extractive industries' projects in countries such as Nicaragua,[51] Paraguay,[52] or Ecuador[53] without the need for exceptional resort to supplementing concepts.[54] As noted by the Inter-American Court of Human Rights in a leading case:

> the close ties of indigenous people with the land must be recognized and understood as the fundamental basis of their cultures, their spiritual life, their integrity, and their economic survival. For indigenous communities, relations to the land are *not merely a matter of possession and production but a material and spiritual element which they must fully enjoy, even to preserve their cultural legacy and transmit it to future generations.*[55]

The Court used Article 21 of the American Convention on Human Rights,[56] which recognises the right to property, as a suitable vehicle to give effect to the relationship between an indigenous people and its ancestral land. But, in truth, there is a part of incommensurability between the two notions. The

51 See *Mayagna (Sumo) Awas Tingni Community v. Nicaragua*, ICtHR Series C No. 79, Judgment (31 August 2001).

52 See *Case of Sawhoyamaxa Indigenous Community v Paraguay*, ICtHR Series C No 146 (29 March 2006), paragraph 118 (indigenous conception of property).

53 See *Indigenous People Kichwa of Sarayaku v. Ecuador*, ICtHR Series C No. 245, Judgment (merits and compensation)(27 June 2012), paragraphs 145–147 (indigenous conception of property).

54 See above n. 49 and 50.

55 *Awas Tingni v. Nicaragua*, above n. 51, para 149 (italics added).

56 American Convention on Human Rights, 22 November 1969, 1144 U.N.T.S. 123.

conclusions of the Court in this and subsequent cases, most notably requiring the respondent State to integrate such communal entitlements into the land register and, more generally, into the legal order, suggest that the relationship between an indigenous people and its ancestral land needs to be reduced or re-coded before it can be given effect in a legal system akin to what Weber called European law, with all its diversity but also its – in some respects converging – ontology.

Beyond the specific illustration of property, the deliberate attempt to detach law from at least certain metaphysical conceptions of nature as well as the efforts to conceptualise law as a pure technique, however useful, also have implications for the role of law in prompting, sustaining and potentially managing the massive human impacts on the Earth system unveiled by the Anthropocene narrative. From the perspective of the research agenda proposed here, this conclusion raises questions relating to the ways in which law and metaphysical conceptions of nature may be interwoven with each other, to the processes through which law has been detached from nature and the implications of such detachment, and to the (un)desirability and potential avenues through which the two could be reconnected. As discussed next, the detachment of law from nature relies on an important yet implicit assumption, namely that human action could never become a nature-changing force of geological proportions. Indeed, the assumption of a natural 'theatre' that is external and immutable is deeply ingrained in virtually all legal concepts, as it was in most ethical systems until the second half of the XX century. However, the Anthropocene narrative emphasises that this assumption is questionable, and it calls for a redefinition of the assumptions on which legal concepts are based.

3.3 The Horizon of Law in the Anthropocene

3.3.1 *Hans Jonas and the Horizon of Ethics*

The work of the German philosopher Hans Jonas[57] provides a useful starting-point to explore a general question relating to a major and implicit assumption underpinning our legal concepts.

The new far-reaching powers that humans have conquered through the development of technology, and their implications for nuclear warfare,

57 H. Jonas, *In Search of an Ethics for the Technological Age* (Chicago IL: University of Chicago Press, 1984) (translation by H. Jonas and David Herr of Jonas' book originally published in German: *Das Prinzip Verantwortung. Versuch einer Ethik für die technologische Zivilisation* (Frankfurt am Main: Suhrkamp, 1979)); H. Jonas, 'Philosophy at the End of the Century: Survey of its Past and Future' (1994) 61/4 *Social Research* 815 (see, particularly, Jonas' discussion of the ecological crisis starting at page 826).

ecological degradation or genetic engineering, exceed the horizon of traditional ethics. Jonas' work – much as the Anthropocene narrative today – highlighted that irrespective of the particular strand of ethics, it has been assumed that the normative guidance provided by ethical principles mainly concerned contemporary relations among humans living in a society. This is not to say that ethical principles cannot be adapted or extended beyond human relations (e.g. relations with different entities in nature) or beyond contemporaneity (e.g. relations to humans in the past or the future). But the immensity of the new powers acquired by humans and their potentially devastating effects on the Earth system as a whole called, in Jonas' opinion, for much more. At the very least, it called for an ethics specifically (rather than tangentially) concerned with the implications of such unprecedented powers and based on a reformulated understanding of responsibility.

Jonas' point is of great relevance also for other normative constructs such as law. Much like ethics, law does not merely seek to reflect reality through a variety of concepts but also to norm it. In other words, law – as ethics – is not a mere mirror of reality but a purposeful mirror. It seeks to both represent and orient behaviour. In point of fact, the main reason why it seeks to accurately represent reality is because it attempts to norm it. In this context, the newly acquired powers of humans have to be reflected to some extent in ethical and legal concepts, both for accuracy and normative (governance) purposes. Yet, as noted earlier in this essay, the prevailing approach followed by most legal systems is to address the externalities of the very transactions that have led, at least in part, to the Anthropocene. The organisation of the transactions' core has only been comprehensively reshaped in rare occasions, such as the ban of slavery and forced labour, or in contexts where the re-organisation has led to no less severe impacts on both humans and the natural environment, such as in communist planned economic production.

3.3.2 *The Task for Law*

Taking due account of human technological powers entailed, for H. Jonas, revisiting the foundations of ethics to ingrain an unprecedented level of responsibility on humans. Broadly speaking, the task of law in the Anthropocene is no different than that of ethics: it has to ingrain the unprecedented implications of human technological power in its foundational concepts. Much like for ethics, the question is not merely whether existing legal concepts can be extended and adjusted to reflect the new human condition but, more generally, whether new legal ontologies must be developed that are specifically (not just tangentially) concerned with the geological implications of human powers.

An additional difficulty faced by law arises from its social regulatory function. As noted by Jonas, it is not for philosophy to work out what he called the 'actual articles of a possible peace pact' between mind (i.e. human technological power) and nature, but only to give the general argument and direction. The specificities would be the task of 'practical experts' and:

> [a]ll the sciences concerning nature and human beings, concerning economics, politics and society, must cooperate in drafting a planetary statement of condition along with suggestions for arriving at a budget balanced between human beings and nature.[58]

By its very function, law would be in the important and difficult position of translating such specific approaches and practical steps. It would continue to be a technology, but with different goals and foundations. Indeed, in order to do so, much like ethics for its own task (setting the overall direction), we must find an appropriate legal language, i.e. a set of interrelated legal concepts capable of spelling out the new (or the diversity of new) programme(s), or we must sufficiently reformulate the prevailing legal ontologies.

Developing appropriate legal concepts may not merely consist in adding some new concepts or layers of concepts (e.g. the precautionary approach or other 'principles'[59]) or in fine-tuning some old ones (e.g. the extension of the concept of damage to cover also the so-called 'pure ecological damage'[60]). It may require to entirely redefine some concepts (e.g. as suggested by the example of property, discussed in the previous section) or, more fundamentally, redefine the entire legal cartography or language used to represent and norm the world, establishing new concepts and relations among them.

Ingraining in the law the unprecedented level of responsibility arising for humans raises several questions from the perspective of the present research agenda starting with the identification of the most relevant legal concepts and implications, and ending with the potential redefinition of the entire legal language or ontology. The main initial question is indeed whether existing legal concepts adequately translate the unprecedented level of responsibility

58 Jonas (1994), above n. 57, at 830.

59 This seems to be, however, the approach suggested in some of the environmental law literature. See e.g. Robinson (2012) and (2014), above n. 16.

60 For an overview of approaches taken in international and comparative law, see M. Anderson, A. Boyle (eds.), *Environmental Damage in International and Comparative Law. Problems of Definition and Valuation* (Oxford University Press, 2002)

of humans in the Anthropocene. Depending on the answer, the next question would concern the identification of the concepts that could be added or reworked (expanded, redefined, suppressed) and the exploration of the interactions among such revisited concepts and the wider legal order. In the end, what is at stake is whether a new legal ontology, a more precise language, should be developed in order to fully reflect the new level of responsibility of humans. Brought back to our current understanding of the role of law with respect to the environment, what is called into question is the sufficiency of addressing our ecological crisis through the sole prism of negative externalities or external (stochastic) shocks, which is the prevailing prism in environmental law.

3.4 Revisiting Foundational Concepts

3.4.1 *Transactions-Externalities: The External Logic of Environmental Law*

The way in which the legal protection of the environment emerged and developed mainly from the 1950s onwards clearly conveys the assumption that the environment is an external object.[61]

Whether it is through personal-injury based techniques (e.g. through tort law doctrines of nuisance or civil law doctrines of *abus de droit*, and more recently environmental liability and human rights litigation) or through impact limitation techniques (e.g. environmental impact assessments, environmental permitting, zoning and protection of designated areas, pollution limitation standards, taxation, or market mechanisms), the assumption is that the legal system first organises social processes, such as defining subjects, rights, duties, devolution of powers, general taxation, corporate structures, economic freedoms, labour relations, horizontal relations (e.g. tort and contract law), etc., and only then it adds a layer of regulation aimed at protecting the environment. It sets bounds to (it 'regulates') the effects of a pre-established system.

In order to preserve the foundational legal categories and their goals, such an additional layer may even be organised on the basis of the very same concepts used to pursue the implicit value system ingrained in law (e.g. the quest for growth and efficiency).[62] By way illustration, law may grant property rights ('sovereign rights') over the resources located in the exclusive economic zones

61 There is no major historical account looking at the development of domestic environmental law across countries. With some rare exceptions (e.g. R. Lazarus, *The Making of Environmental Law* (Chicago IL: University of Chicago Press, 2004, focusing on the United States), one must resort to the initial chapters of environmental law textbooks in the relevant jurisdictions.

62 See e.g. D. Grinlinton, P. Taylor (eds), *Property Rights and Sustainability: The Evolution of Property Rights to meet Ecological Challenges* (Leiden: Martinus Nijhoff, 2011) (the

of States[63] in order to strengthen the incentives of coastal States to protect such resources (e.g. fisheries), or it may create rights to pollute within tolerable levels, as for a variety of allowances relating to the emissions of sulphur dioxide[64] or carbon dioxide[65] to reduce pollution while achieving efficiency. In both cases, the implications of property (the possibility of appropriation or the externalities of using property in certain ways) are addressed by resorting to an extension of property concepts (sovereign rights or rights to pollute). This approach contrasts with the possibility of reverting to other notions of property or reformulating its very understanding, as discussed in section 3.2.2, to integrate respect for nature and future generations.

Such a choice may be entirely legitimate if its implications for the overall operation of a legal order or for society are fully understood as well as deliberately and legitimately chosen. But even in more traditional forms of environmental regulation, such as the requirement of a prior environmental impact assessment, the approach remains supplemental in that it simply adds a requirement for the conduct of an activity that is otherwise fully organised through the laws relating to corporate structures, economic freedoms, property rights, contractual arrangements, labour relations, and others. Such structures, freedoms, rights and arrangements are not themselves reformulated. The corporate form keeps its personality and governance arrangements, protecting shareholders from creditors of the corporation as well as corporate assets from shareholders and their creditors. Economic freedoms tend to be extended rather than restricted by the privatisation of activities formerly deemed to be public in nature, such as utilities or even security. Property rights are multiplied and found to govern more and more parcels of reality, including a clean atmosphere or clean water or still 'natural capital'. Contractual arrangements become increasingly standardised and complex, leaving limited bargaining power to some parties and largely substituting for public action.

These are but some illustrations of the legal organisation that Max Weber considered to be initially conducive to the rise of capitalism and later

---

contributors to this edited volume offer a critical perspective on property rights as tool for environmental protection and discuss different adjustments and reformulations).

63 Under the international law of sea, as codified by the United Nations Convention on the Law of the Sea, 10 December 1982, 1833 UNTS 397, Part V, coastal States have 'sovereign rights', i.e. exclusive jurisdiction, over the exploitation of natural resources in the water column extending up to 200 nautical miles from their baselines.

64 See G. Chan, R. Stavins, R. Stowe, R. Sweeney, 'The SO2 allowance-trading system and the Clean Air Act Amendments of 1990: Reflections on 20 years of policy innovation' (2012) 65 *National Tax Journal* 419.

65 See D. Freestone, C. Streck (eds.), *Legal Aspects of Carbon Trading* (Oxford University Press, 2009).

promoted and increasingly shaped by it. It is premised on the idea of the market as a spontaneous regulator and, more fundamentally, on the idea of efficiency (maximising utility at the lowest cost). Cost internalisation of negative externalities through market mechanisms partakes in this approach. But so does environmental and social regulation, as it is now conceived, namely as an additional layer of law targeting the effects of separately organised transactions. We have lost sight of how idiosyncratic and culturally-situated the growth and efficiency-based legal organisation of society and its relations with nature are. Comparative law but also non-legal disciplines such as historiography and anthropology could help to broaden the perspective that we have on our legal concepts and conceptions through the essay of entirely different legal ontologies and of how the relations between humans and nature are organised in them.

3.4.2 *Illustrations: Conceptions of Sovereignty and Causality*

As before, providing some illustrations of the distinction between legal concepts addressing the externality and those that capture the transaction's core may be useful to clarify its practical implications.

The first illustration is provided by the concept of State sovereignty in international law. States have powers over the organisation of their economic activities and the exploitation of their natural resources within their territory or jurisdiction. Such a distribution of powers, which was a major cause of the collective action problem leading to increasing emissions of greenhouse gases,[66] is based on a distribution of political power legally expressed through the concept of sovereignty. States are 'sovereign' in that they are independent from all other States and have the full and exclusive exercise of public prerogatives within their territory.[67] Unrestricted use of such powers may have deleterious

66 See the study by S. Barrett, *Environment and Statecraft* (Oxford University Press, 2003) (discussing how the political organization expressed by the concept of sovereignty limits cooperation).

67 See *Island of Palmas Case* (*or Miangas*) (*United States v Netherlands*), Award (4th April 1928), II RIAA 829 (where the sole arbitrator, the Swiss Max Huber, stated the most influential understanding of the concept of territorial sovereignty, still valid today: 'Sovereignty in the relations between States signifies independence. Independence in regard to a portion of the globe is the right to exercise therein, to the exclusion of any other State, the functions of a State. The development of the national organisation of States during the last few centuries and, as a corollary, the development of international law, have established this principle of the exclusive competence of the State in regard to its own territory in such a way as to make it the point of departure in settling most questions that concern international relations', at 838).

effects on the environment of other States or beyond national jurisdiction. As a result, the exercise of such powers has been subject to an additional layer of regulation at the international level, including norms such as the prevention principle, the principle of cooperation or the requirement to conduct a prior environmental impact assessment.[68] In this approach, the environment is an external object for the protection of which the exercise of sovereignty is restricted to some extent.[69] To move beyond the current binary approach whereby sovereignty is first asserted and then some limits to its exercise are added, the very concept of sovereignty would need to be shaken to its roots. Some scholars have argued in favour of a reconceptualisation of sovereignty as a form of stewardship or trusteeship, not merely for the benefit of a State's population, as in mainstream democratic theory, but also for the benefit of those beyond it.[70] The very need to respect the environment would no longer be an *ad hoc* limitation of sovereignty but an integral part of it, much like in the example of communal property discussed in section 3.2.2.

Another example of a basic legal concept that is challenged by the Anthropocene narrative is that of 'causality'. There are different theories of causality in both domestic (e.g. tort law) and international law (e.g. State responsibility) and they all convey, whether explicitly or implicitly, a value judgment or normative choice of what consequences are to be legally attributed to a given act/omission of an agent. Such value judgments are culturally-situated but they also respond to practical considerations. In a traditional causation of fact principle or 'causalité adéquate' test, some consequences of actions would escape attribution if the link between a specific tortious act and the injury suffered by the victim cannot be established at the relevant standard of proof (e.g. preponderance of the evidence). This understanding of causality could be expanded to give more room to scientific and fairness considerations. Ronald Dworkin has highlighted the normative dimensions of such an extension by

68 See Rio Declaration on Environment and Development, 13 June 1992, UN Doc. A/CONF.151/26, principles 2 (prevention), 17 (environmental impact assessment), 18–19 (cooperation). For a detailed commentary of this foundational instrument see J. E. Viñuales (ed.), *The Rio Declaration on Environment and Development. A Commentary* (Oxford University Press, 2015).

69 This is the thesis expounded by N. Shrijver, *Sovereignty over Natural Resources. Balancing Rights and Duties* (Cambridge University Press, 1997).

70 For two prominent examples see F. Francioni, 'Realism, Utopia and the Future of International Environmental Law', in A. Cassese (ed.), *Realizing Utopia. The Future of International Law* (Oxford University Press, 2012), at 442–460; E. Benvenisti, 'Sovereigns as Trustees of Humanity: On the Acocuntability of States to Foreign Stateholders (2013) 107/2 *American Journal of International Law* 295.

reference to the imaginary case of Mrs. Sorenson[71] (conceptually reflecting the well-known case *Sindell v. Abbott Laboratories*[72]) where the traditional rule of liability requiring causation is overcome by a theory of 'market-share liability', under which each proved contributor to the problem is liable to the extent of its contribution, measured by its market share, even if a causality link with the specific damage suffered by the victim is not established. Market-share liability is a legal approach to fill a gap left by the conventional requirements of causation. Its legal nature has been debated,[73] but its operation would allow for a legal extension (based on a normative choice) of a factual relationship that cannot be fully established scientifically. However, applying such an expanded conception of causality (where, in fact, the tortious act is considered to be that of a group of defendants taken together, which is then causally related to the injury) in the context of Earth system change remains particularly challenging because the group deemed to commit a tortious act is not easily identifiable (it would include, at the very least, portions of past and present generations, with different sectors involved) and the injury itself cannot easily be attributed to a major environmental disruption (e.g. whereas climate change increases the frequency of several extreme weather events, attributing a specific event to it – e.g. the hurricane that took place on a given day of May – remains scientifically difficult). In many ways, the main legal shield still protecting those groups and countries responsible for climate change-inducing emissions is the prevailing understanding of causality. As with the concept of sovereignty, a

71 See R. Dworkin, *Justice in Robes* (Cambridge MA: Harvard University Press, 2006), at 143 ('Mrs. Sorenson suffered from rheumatoid arthritis and for many years took a generic drug – inventum – to relieve her suffering. During that period inventum was manufactured and marketed under different trade names by eleven different pharmaceutical companies. In fact the drug had serious and undisclosed side-effects, of which the manufacturers should have known, and Mrs. Sorenson suffered permanent cardiac damage from taking it. She was unable to prove which manufacturer's pills [...] had actually injured her. She sued all the drug companies who had manufactured inventum, together, and her lawyers argued that each of them was liable to her in proportion to its share of the market in the drug over the years of her treatment. The drug companies replied that the plaintiff's request was entirely novel and contradicted the long established premise of tort law that no one is liable for injury he has not been shown to have caused. They said that since Mrs. Sorenson could not show that any particular defendant had injured her or even manufactured any of the inventum she took, she could recover against none of them.').

72 *Sindell v. Abbott Labs*, 607 P.2d 924 (Cal. 1980).

73 M. A. Geistfeld, 'The Doctrinal Unity of Alternative Liability and Market-Share Liability' (2006) 155 *University of Pennsylvania Law Review* 447, at 449–452 (discussing conceptions of market-share liability as risk-based liability or as a more complex expression of damage/causation-based liability).

reconceptualisation of the legal principle of causality would have to ingrain the complexity of natural processes within law, that is capturing complexity as understood in science (e.g. in climate modelling), where minor differences in the initial conditions can lead to very different outcomes the longer the process unfolds. But as suggested by the market share liability theory, such a reconceptualisation is not necessarily reliant on the scientific ability to establish traditional causality and could also be addressed through a normative extension allowing the legally-redefined causality link to cover more ground.

Importantly, the challenges that the Anthropocene poses to the concept of sovereignty and the principle of causality also illustrate another wider problem that any reconceptualisation attempt is bound to face, namely the imbrication of legal concepts. Indeed, legal concepts, and particularly the most foundational ones, can only be defined in relation to each other. Taken together, their imbrication amounts to a legal ontology, a specific representation of reality, as discussed in section 3.3.2. Reconceptualising sovereignty or causality is likely to change many other areas of a legal order such as the understanding of responsibility/liability which, in turn, is likely to change the understanding of duties or obligations (e.g. a new tort based on risk has been considered as a corollary of the extension of causality in market-share liability) as well as of rights (rights of recovery but also of action) which, in turn, may also redefine the concept of subject (recognising an obligation towards future generations or parts of the environment or granting to these entities the right to bring an action would amount to creating at least partial subjects of law). Whether the reconceptualisation process starts at one or the other end (e.g. whether it starts with the concept of obligation or that of subject), the interconnectedness of legal concepts cannot be overlooked.

From the perspective of this essay, the foregoing examples provide a further illustration of the differences between an external logic, which currently prevails in the making of environmental law, and the possibility of redefining certain foundational legal concepts to ingrain nature within them. At the same time, they raise a number of important questions relating to the areas of environmental law where the external logic appears insufficient to address the challenges of the Anthropocene as well as to the most suitable approaches to rise to such challenges. Specifically, one question is whether conventional environmental law can be enhanced (I will discuss later in this essay the attempts to develop 'adaptive environmental law') or whether, at least in some areas, a reformulation of foundational legal concepts is necessary. To the extent that the latter approach may be explored, particular attention should be paid to the imbrications or 'side-effects' of different reformulations of a foundational concept.

More clearly reflecting the complexities of nature and the unprecedented responsibility of humans are not the only tasks for law in the Anthropocene. Neither the responsibility for prompting and sustaining the Anthropocene nor the impacts (positive or negative) of the challenges posed by this new epoch are spread equally across the entire human race. There are differences and inequalities within the apparently homogeneous category of 'humans' as a geological force, and they raise a question of distributive justice for which law also needs to account.

Part 3: Accounting for Inequality

1 *Preliminary Observations*

The need to address questions of inequality and redistribution within the Anthropocene narrative highlights the fundamental role of social sciences and humanities, including law, in understanding our new condition. Indeed, natural science accounts of the Anthropocene have been oblivious or insufficiently sensitive to what lies beneath an analytical category such as 'humankind' or 'human systems' or, still, 'human agency'. In the attempts at developing models that take into account the interactions between natural processes and humans, the latter are taken as a single homogeneous variable, even by those modelling efforts that seek to provide higher resolution to the interactions taking place within the Earth system.[74] This difficulty has been highlighted in a number of contributions from social scientists, such as those of Andreas Malm and Alf Hornborg,[75] Christophe Bonneuil and Jean-Baptiste Fressoz,[76] and Frank Biermann and colleagues.[77]

---

74 See e.g. the 'Bretherton Diagram' where 'human activities' are integrated as an additional component or cycle of a socio-ecological system (*Earth System Science Overview. A Program for Global Change*, NASA Science Advisory Committee, 1986, at 19) or newer models with a higher resolution of the human variable (F. Berkes, J. Folke, C. Colding (eds.), *Navigating Social-Ecological Systems. Building Resilience for Complexity and Change* (Cambridge University Press, 2003), or E. Bennett, G. D. Peterson, L. J. Gordon, 'Understanding relationships among multiple ecosystem services' (2009) 12/12 *Ecology Letters*1394), all referred to in Bonneuil/Fressoz, above n. 1, at 48–49.

75 A. Malm, A. Hornborg, 'The geology of mankind? A critique of the Anthropocene narrative' (2014) 1/1 *The Anthropocene Review* 62.

76 See Bonneuil/Fressoz, above n. 1.

77 See F. Biermann et al., 'Down to Earth: Contextualizing the Anthropocene' (2016) 39 *Global Environmental Change* 341 (and the other contributions to this special issue devoted to the Anthropocene).

The main tenets of this critique concern: (i) the dominance of natural science approaches in the Anthropocene narrative; (ii) the inability of such approaches to capture important and even decisive intra-species inequalities among humans; (iii) the higher responsibility of early industrialised countries, particularly the United Kingdom and the United States, and their elites in the advent of the Anthropocene; (iv) the wide diversities in those who have benefited from the results of technology and those who have suffered from their adverse effects; and (v) the implications of not recognising such disparities for the attempts at taking action to address the root causes of the Anthropocene.

As with the previous analysis of the disconnection between law and nature, it is important to introduce a detour through some social science accounts of the Anthropocene, both to identify the implications for law and legal analysis and to relate the ensuing legal questions to a wider and integrative research agenda encompassing other disciplines.

2 *A Finer-grained Analysis of the Human Variable*

The use of 'humankind' as an analytical category fails to capture the importance of historical contingency in human processes and thereby in the impact of humans even at the aggregate level of a geological force. Reconnecting conceptually human and natural history calls for different levels of analysis, some of which are widely overlooked by the natural science approaches to the Anthropocene. At this level, the disconnection between natural and human history discussed earlier in this essay is useful to show that human agency is not fully determined by natural causes. Human behaviour is not fully determined either biologically or environmentally. However, introducing elements of historicity and contingency in the Anthropocene narrative does not amount to preserving the disconnection, as natural processes remain important variables in shaping human agency and, perhaps more importantly in this specific context, contingent historical factors may be found at the origin of the human processes – the Industrial Revolution – that have prompted the Anthropocene. In discussing some examples of historical contingencies that have been instrumental in triggering the Industrial Revolution, my purpose is to highlight the need for a finer-grained approach to the connection between humans and nature in the Anthropocene narrative. As I will discuss next, some significant contributions to historiography and social science suggest that historical contingency has played a major role in shaping the type of 'world-systems'[78]

78 For a concise overview of Wallerstein's analytical approach see I. Wallerstein, *World System Analysis: An Introduction* (Durham NC: Duke University Press, 2004). The full extent of Wallerstein's theory was developed in three main volumes: *The Modern World-System*,

capable of explaining (i) why the Industrial Revolution took off in the United Kingdom and Western Europe, and greatly accelerated after the Second World War, and (ii) the profound differences among countries in terms of both historical responsibility for and exposure to the risks of the Anthropocene.

One such contribution to the understanding of the origins of the Industrial Revolution in the UK and some parts of Western Europe is the study of the American historian Kenneth Pomeranz entitled *The Great Divergence*.[79] Pomeranz seeks to overcome what he sees as a divide in historical accounts of the origins of the Industrial Revolution between two polarised theses, where 'either a Europe-centered world system carrying out essential primitive accumulation [of capital] overseas or endogenous European growth [are] called upon to explain almost everything'.[80] He adopts a comparative method assessing the similar overall conditions prevailing in certain areas as late as 1750, particularly England and the Yangzi Delta region, as potentially conducive for what became the Industrial Revolution. He then asks 'Why wasn't England the Yangzi Delta?' and, conversely 'Why wasn't the Yangzi Delta England?'[81] His detailed and elaborate answer, which occupies the rest of the book, points to two main differences between the subsequent paths followed by the two regions, namely the fortuitous availability of great reserves of coal in the UK (that could substitute for forests) and the 'natural bounty' made available through trade flows of raw materials against manufactures between the UK and its colonies or former colonies (that could largely substitute for land and relied on slavery). These two factors made possible a capital and manufacture intensive path, with a growing population fed by natural resources from overseas grown/extracted by slaves. By contrast, the development of the East Asian hinterland retained the resources of these peripheral areas, which were therefore not available to fuel a similar trajectory in the Yangzi Delta. As noted by Pomeranz:

> China's Lower Yangzi [...] had increasing trouble selling enough cloth and importing enough food and timber to sustain either proto-industrial

---

vol. I: Capitalist Agriculture and the Origins of the European World-Economy in the Sixteenth Century (New York/London: Academic Press, 1974); *The Modern World-System, vol. II: Mercantilism and the Consolidation of the European World-Economy, 1600–1750* (New York/London: Academic Press, 1980); *The Modern World-System, vol. III: The Second Great Expansion of the Capitalist World-Economy, 1730–1840's* (San Diego: Academic Press, 1989).

79 K. Pomeranz, *The Great Divergence: China, Europe and the Making of the Modern World Economy* (Princeton NJ: Princeton University Press, 2000).

80 *Ibid.*, at 5.

81 *Ibid.*, at 13.

> growth or the relatively high living standards of its workers. This was not because of any internal "flaw" in the region but because the areas it had traded with were undergoing their own population and proto-industrial booms and so were becoming less complementary to it.[82]

For present purposes, the main question is not whether Pomeranz's analysis provides a more accurate picture of the origins of the Industrial Revolution than the other polarised theses that he seeks to overcome. Rather, it is the need to resort to historical analysis and look at certain contingencies, such as the availability of coal and the asymmetric imperial trade, to explain the emergence of the thermo-industrial revolution that prompted the Anthropocene.

In addition, the asymmetry presented by one of these contingencies is of critical importance to highlight that it is not the entire humankind that drove and benefitted from the industrial processes underpinning the Anthropocene but only a highly privileged portion of it, whose location has varied over the last two centuries from England and some countries of Western Europe, to the United States and Japan as well as some areas of the former Soviet Bloc after the Second World War, to China and some other 'emerging' economies in the last decades. By contrast, large portions of the world population suffered from the colonial and post-colonial political asymmetry that enabled the Industrial Revolution and the post-1945 Great Acceleration and hardly partook in the resulting benefits. To capture such disparities, an analytical approach with much higher resolution that the one proposed by the natural science narrative of the Anthropocene is required. And such disparities are important to understand the Anthropocene not only from the perspective of the latter's impact on different peoples around the world but also because, without such disparities, the Industrial Revolution may not have been possible. As noted at the beginning of this essay, the legal organisation of empires and nation-States as well as of productions processes was part of the technologies that prompted the Anthropocene. In an important critique of Crutzen's standard narrative of the Anthropocene, Swedish human ecologists Andreas Malm and Alf Hornborg argue that:

> uneven distribution [of resources and wealth] is a condition for the very existence of modern, fossil-fuel technology [...] These technologies are an index of capital accumulation, privileged resource consumption, and the displacement of both work and environmental loads. After more than 20 years, we still tend to imagine "technological progress" as nothing but

82 *Ibid.*, at 22.

> the magic wand of ingenuity which, with no necessary political or moral implications elsewhere, will solve our local problems of sustainability.[83]

Critical accounts of the dynamics of the Industrial Revolution, particularly of the inequalities on which it relied, raise the wider question of the origins and workings of capitalism. However polemic, such accounts provide powerful analytical tools to understand human agency leading to the Anthropocene and, more specifically, the role of law within it.

The work of American sociologist Immanuel Wallerstein on 'world-system analysis'[84] is particularly illuminating in this regard because it is capable of linking a given organisation of a world-system, such as the UK-dominated one that prevailed from the late XVIII to the beginning of the XX century, with an ensuing social and ecological footprint. Bonneuil and Fressoz review several contributions that, relying on the concept of world-systems, have tried to clarify the ecological implications of different production systems, particularly during the British-led Industrial Revolution and the US-led Great Acceleration.[85] This ecological footprint can be calculated by reference to concepts such as 'ghost or incorporated hectares' (i.e. the number of hectares necessary to produce a given good or raw material) or 'ecological unequal exchange' (i.e. exchanges of goods that require far less land or have a far lower ecological footprint against goods with far higher land requirements or ecological footprints). By way of illustration, Hornborg has estimated that, in 1850, an exchange of £1000 of textile manufactured in Manchester against £1000 of

83 Malm/Hornborg, above n. 75, at 64.

84 See above n. 78.

85 Bonneuil/Fressoz, above n. 1, chapter 10, referring a number of interdisciplinary studies: H. Schandl, N. Schulz, 'Changes in the United Kingdom's natural relations in terms of society's metabolism and land-use from 1850 to the present day' (2002) 41 *Ecological Economics* 203; A. Hornborg, C. L. Crumley (ed.), *The World System and the Earth System* (Walnut Creek CA: Left Coast Press, 2006); M. Fischer-Kowalski, H. Haberl (eds.), *Socioecological Transitions and Global Change: Trajectories of Social Metabolism and Land Use* (Cheltenham: Edward Elgar, 2007); J. B. Foster, B. Clark, 'Ecological imperialism and the global metabolic rift: Unequal exchange and the guano/nitrates trade' (2009) 50 *International Journal of Comparative Sociology* 311; J. B. Foster, B. Clark, R. York, *The Ecological Rift. Capitalism War on the Earth* (Monthly Review Press, 2010); A. Hornborg, *Global Ecology and Unequal Exchange. Fetishism in a Zero-Sum World* (London: Routledge, 2013); A. Hornborg, 'Ecological economics, Marxism, and technological progress: Some explorations of the conceptual foundations of theories of ecological unequal exchange' (2014) 105 *Ecological Economics* 11; J. B. Foster, H. Holleman, 'The theory of unequal ecological exchange: A Marx-Odum dialectic' (2014) 41 *Journal of Peasant Studies* 199; J. W. Moore, *Capitalism in the Web of Life* (London: Verso, 2015); A. Malm, *Fossil Capital. The Rise of Steam-Power and the Roots of Global Warming* (London: Verso, 2016).

cotton produced in the US was highly unequal in ecological terms because the US cotton required 6000 times more land than the English goods.[86] A similar estimation concerns the increasing UK net imports of biomass, which were multiplied by a factor of six over the period from 1855 to 1930.[87] The ecological footprint of the Great Acceleration is also immense and highly uneven. In a study published in 2014,[88] a group of Austrian scientists showed that since the 1950s, global material consumption (an aggregate variable of all materials processed in an economy, except for water and air, including biomass, fossil energy resources, metals, industrial minerals, construction minerals, and other traded products) has increased faster (by a factor of 3.7) than population (by a factor of 2.7). The distribution of this increase, both in the aggregate and in per capita measures, clearly shows striking levels of inequality in the consumption/use of such materials. Up to 1990, the West and the Soviet block amounted together to over 50% of globally extracted materials. Over the period 1950–2010, annual per capita consumption in the West was three times (14.8 tonnes) that in Sub-Saharan Africa (4.8 tonnes). Starting in 2000, Asia (particularly China) overtook the West in its global share of resource use, although not in per capita terms.

These are but some measures of inequality relevant for the assessment of the relative ecological footprint of countries, groups of countries, and populations. But they clearly convey the message that inequality is deeply present in human agency, and that using 'humankind' as an aggregate variable is not only unfair but also inaccurate.

3 *Law and Inequality in the Anthropocene*

3.1 Overview

A number of legal developments enabled or facilitated the industrial trajectory of the different hegemons and beneficiaries of world-systems, to adopt the terminology of Wallerstein.

In addition to the oft-cited consolidation of unified management, limited liability and share tradability as a major advantages of new business organisations,[89] the legal questions relevant for the understanding of these

86 Hornborg 2013, above n. 85, at 85–91.

87 Schandl/Schulz, above n. 85, at 215.

88 A. Schaffartzik et al., 'The global metabolic transition: Regional patterns and trends of global material flows, 1950–2010' (2014) 26 *Global Environmental Change* 87.

89 On the origins of industrial corporations see: S. Williston, 'History of the Law of Business Corporations before 1800' (1888) 2/3–4 *Harvard Law Review* 105 (part 1), 149 (part 2); A. Berle, G. Means, *The Modern Corporation and Private Property* (New York: Macmillan, 1932) (classic account of the foundations of corporate law stressing the separation

trajectories would include the protection of the assets of companies against the creditors of shareholders,[90] the legal organisation of labour relations,[91] the accommodation through compensation of the impacts of industrial processes,[92] and more generally an international legal order allowing for the threat or the use of force,[93] downplaying the validity of the territorial title of non-European political entities[94] (with some exceptions, particularly in the Americas), enabling colonial exploitation of natural resources and, later on,

---

between ownership and control of corporate affairs); R. E. Seavoy, *The origins of the American business corporation 1784–1855* (Westport, Conn.: Greenwood Press, 1982) (paying particular attention to corporate law in New York); W. G. Roy, *Socialising Capital: The Rise of the Large Industrial Corporation in America* (Princeton NJ: Princeton University Press, 1997) (analysing the quasi-public origins of major corporations); T. W. Guinnane et al., 'Pouvoir et proprieté dans l'entreprise: Pour une histoire international des sociétés à responsabilité limitée' (2008) 63/1 *Annales. Histoire. Sciences Sociales* 73 (arguing that the diffusion of the corporation as a form of business organization has been overestimated, and focusing on other forms of limited liability organisations in France, Germany, the UK and the US).

90 See e.g. H. Hansmann, R. Kraakman, R. Squire, 'Law and the Rise of the Firm' (2005/2006) 119 *Harvard Law Review* 1335.

91 See e.g. O. Kahn-Freund, 'Legal Framework', in A. Flanders, H. A. Clegg (eds.), *The System of Industrial Relations in Great Britain: its History, Law and Institutions* (Oxford: Blackwell, 1954), at 42–127; O. Kahn-Freund, *Labour Relations: Heritage and Adjustment* (Oxford University Press, 1979); M. Linder, *The Employment Relationship in Anglo-American Law: A Historical Perspective* (New York: Greenwood, 1989); J. Le Goff, *Du silence à la parole. Une histoire du droit du travail des années 1830 à nos jours* (Rennes: Presses universitaires de Rennes, 2004); A. Supiot, *Critique du droit du travail* (Paris: Presses universitaires de France, 2007).

92 See e.g. J. F. Brenner, 'Nuisance Law and the Industrial Revolution' (1974) 3/2 *Journal of Legal Studies* 403; A. E. Dingle, 'The Monster Nuisance of All. Landowners, Alkali Manufacturers, and Air Pollution, 1828–1864' (1982) 35/4 *Economic History Review* 529; B. Pontin, 'Tort Law and Victorian Governement Growth: the historiographical significance of tort law in the shadow of chemical pollution' (1998) 18/4 *Oxford Journal of Legal Studies* 661; G. Massard-Guilbaud, *Histoire de la pollution industrielle en France, 1789–1914* (Paris: EHESS, 2010); J.-B. Fressoz, 'Payer pour polluer: l'industrie chimique et la compensation des dommages environnementaux, 1800–1850' (2013) 28/1 *Histoire & mesure* 145.

93 See e.g. I. Brownlie, *International Law and the Use of Force by States* (Oxford: Clarendon Press, 1963), chapter 2 (focusing on the period between 1815 and 1914).

94 In his discussion of the Berlin Conference on the partition of Africa, John Westlake, the then Whewell Professor of International Law at Cambridge, noted that 'it would be going much further, and to a length to which declined to go, if we were to say that, except in the case of unprovoked aggression justifying conquest, an uncivilized population has rights which makes its free consent necessary to the establishment over it of a government possessing international validity [...] Those arrangements [the Berlin act] are not to be construed as denying, because they do not affirm them, the rights of any who are not stipulating parties to the conventions by which they are made. The moral rights of all outside the international society against the several members of that society remain intact

enabling access to natural resources located abroad as well as to markets for manufactured products.[95]

Given space and my own limitations, it would be impossible to cover, even superficially, all these areas of law and their role in prompting and sustaining the industrial processes characterising the Anthropocene. Instead, my purpose in the following sections is to identify three sets of questions that I see as potentially useful directions for legal research into the arrangements underpinning the trajectories and disparities discussed in the previous section. These three sets include questions relating to the legal organisation of production processes (business organisation, labour relations, impacts on third parties) (3.2) and of asymmetric international exchange systems (colonial and post-colonial) (3.3.), as well as the legal expressions given to disparities in historical responsibilities within humankind (as regards reparation for past damages, the representation of future generations, and the contemporary distribution of the benefits/burden of taking action) (3.4.).

3.2 Legal Organisation of Production

3.2.1 *Organising Production for the Industrial Revolution*

The legal organisation of production processes relies heavily (albeit not entirely) on three bodies of norms, namely those structuring the form of business ventures, those addressing the situation of the workforce, and those dealing with the impacts of industrial processes on third parties. In reviewing the development of these bodies of law, a common feature is the priority given to the organisation of production over its adverse effects. Even the regulation of industrial emissions, which seems specifically targeted to such impacts, focused largely on the reparation of injury suffered by third parties rather than on the banning or structuring of the regulated activities. It is only in recent times, particularly in the second half of the XX, that the centre of gravity of law shifted to the reduction of the harm through preventive techniques.

Yet, the desirability of the industrial processes (e.g. chemical industries or electricity production) remained the driving assumption and the limitations on their operation, however hard fought, took the form of either an additional

though they have not and scarcely could have been converted into legal rights', *Chapters on the Principles of International Law* (Cambridge University Press, 1894), at 139–140.

95 See A. Anghie, *Imperialism, Sovereignty and the Making of International Law* (Cambridge University Press, 2004), at 141–162 (discussing the level of priority accorded by colonial powers to the resources of the colonies and, after the First World War, in the context of the mandate system established by the League of Nations, the discoursive emphasis on developing such resources both for the local populations but, in practice, mostly for the benefit of 'the Commerce of the World').

layer of norms dealing with the protection of social rights, affected populations or the environment (see sections 3.2.3 and 3.2.4) or, increasingly, they were shaped as 'regulation', understood as technical standards aimed at fine-tuning and optimising the operation of a (productive) system.[96]

3.2.2 *The Law of Business Organisation*

The law of business organisation experienced significant change starting in the XIX century in both the UK[97] and the US,[98] but also in other countries benefiting from the 'world-systems' established by the hegemon (e.g. Germany[99] or France[100]). Depending on the level of analysis, the trajectories defined by the law of business organisation and their impact vary from one account to the other. Overall, however, it seems clear that the processes unleashed by the Industrial Revolution were enabled by laws providing certain basic features, such as limited liability (whether provided by a corporate form or by another form of business organisation[101]), unified and separate management, tradability of shares and some protections against liquidation of the business entity, whether against the very owners of the entity (or their successors[102]) or against their creditors.[103]

Importantly, a major factor driving the emergence and development of these legal entities was the need to commit the significant amounts of capital required by industrial and infrastructure projects and the idea of setting up

96 For the distinction between 'regulation', in the meaning of self-adjustment or optimization, and *'règlementation'*, understood as the attempt at governing reality in such a way that it pursues certain values, see Supiot, above n. 91, at X–XIII.

97 See Companies Act 1862 (25 & 26 Vict. c. 89). On the process that led to this statute see P. L. Cottrel, *Industrial Finance 1830–1914. The finance and organization of the English manufacturing industry* (London: Routledge, 1980), chapter 3.

98 See Seavoy, above n. 89 (referring to the law of business organisation in New York).

99 *Aktienrechtsnovelle von 1870* (or New Company Act 1870), which was an amendment of the 1861 *Allgemeines Deutsches Handelsgesetzbuch*, which was further reformed in 1884. See N. Horn, 'Aktienrechtliche Unternehmensorganisation in der Hochindustrialisierung (1860–1920)', in N. Horn, J. Kocka (eds.), *Recht und Entwicklung der Grossunternehmen im 19. und frühen 20. Jahrhundert: wirtschafts-, sozial- und rechtshistorische Untersuchungen zur Industrialisierung in Deutschland, Frankreich, England und den USA* (Göttingen: Vandenhoeck & Ruprecht, 1979), at 123–189.

100 *Loi du 24 juillet 1867 sur les sociétés commerciales*. On the process leading to this statute see C. E. Freedeman, *Joint-stock enterprise in France, 1807–1867: From privileged company to modern corporation* (Chapel Hill: University of North Carolina Press, 1970).

101 See Guinnane et al., above n. 89.

102 See M. M. Blair, 'Locking in Capital: What Corporate Law Achieved for Business Organizers in the Nineteenth Century' (2003) 51 *UCLA Law Review* 387.

103 See Hansmann et al., above n. 90.

'chartered' entities was modelled on earlier State-sponsored entities used to pursue colonial interests (e.g. England's East India Company) and/or to manage public monopolies.[104] The economic importance of these new business organisations is well known and does not call for much additional comment. I should add, however, that until quite recently – at least when one considers the history of the Industrial Revolution – the 'social responsibility' of corporations was still understood as the mere maximisation of their profits.[105]

The emergence of corporate social responsibility standards[106] has not changed this picture fundamentally as such standards, to the extent they are indeed implemented, are rarely a driver of the business organisation of a venture.[107] Rather, they operate as (normally non-binding) limitations setting some broad outer limits (regarding human rights, social rights, environmental protection, corruption, etc.) for business action, much in the same way as the two other areas of law to which I now turn, namely labour relations and impact on third parties.

3.2.3 *Structuring Labour Relations*

Labour relations in Britain remained largely unaddressed by statute law until the second half of the XX century. Until the 1960s and 1970s, labour relations were governed essentially by employers and trade unions in what O. Kahn-Freund, a prominent labour lawyer, called 'collective laissez-faire'.[108]

The emergence of this governance approach was hard fought,[109] as for most of the XIX century, trade unions had to face hostile common law courts that considered their aims and action as contrary to economic freedoms (the

104 See Hansmann et al., above n. 90, at 1377 (referring to Holdsworth and Williston); Roy, above n. 89.

105 In the early 1960s, Milton Friedman famously wrote that the social responsibility of business was merely to increase its profits. See M. Friedman, *Capitalism and Freedom* (Chicago IL: University of Chicago Press, 1962), at 155.

106 See A. B. Carroll, 'A History of Corporate Social Responsibility: Concepts and Practices', in A. Crane et al. (eds.), *The Oxford Handbook of Corporate Social Responsibility* (Oxford University Press, 2008), at 19–45.

107 The external dimension of corporate social responsibility, as an additional layer over-imposed on 'normal' business operations, can be contrasted with the focus on social development as an integral dimension of so-called 'social entrepreneurship'. See e.g. A. Nicholls (ed.), *Social Entrepreneurship. New Models of Sustainable Social Change* (Oxford University Press, 2006) and, for an exposition of the principles underlying a prominent example, see M. Yunus, K. Weber, *Building Social Business* (New York: Public Affairs, 2010) (relying on the experience gained by Yunus' founded Grameen bank).

108 Kahn-Freund (1954), above n. 91.

109 For a vivid account of the history of trade unions in Britain see A. Reid, *United We Stand. A History of Britain's Trade Unions* (London: Penguin, 2005).

doctrine of restraint of trade) and exposed strike organisers to potential liability on the basis of several economic torts (conspiracy, inducing breach of contract, interfering with trade or business).[110] As late as 1901, in the *Taff Vale* case, the House of Lords expressed the view that trade unions could be directly sued in tort and held liable for the acts of their officials.[111] In this tense context, the framework for self-regulation was introduced through subsequent statutory interventions in 1871 and 1906 under which trade unions and strike organisers were shielded from the doctrine of restraint of trade and common law economic torts.

In the United States, in the late XIX and early XX century, worker movements faced similar resistance from the judiciary, on the basis of criminal conspiracy charges or through the use of labour injunctions.[112] After the Great Depression, however, the loss of confidence in business leaders and courts as well as the massive protests staged by farmers and workers led to a series of statutory interventions, above all the *National Labor Relations Act* of 1935 (NLRA), which legitimised the use of collective bargaining.[113]

In both countries, economic freedoms were initially and for more than a century used to sustain the asymmetric relation of power, subjecting workers to employers. Economic torts were interpreted in such a way as if worker mobilisation could only hurt employers and national prosperity, overlooking the very reasons why workers mobilised in the first place. In the United States, at the turn from the XIX to the XX century, this tension had crystallised into competing interpretations of the Thirteenth Amendment. Workers saw themselves as subject to a condition of 'involuntary servitude' whereas courts asserted that the Thirteenth Amendment only protected the individual right to resign free from physical coercion.[114] This tension recalls the darker origins of the asymmetry sustained by law, namely slavery, and it connects the stories of the US and the UK in that, as argued by K. Pomeranz, the latter was able to overcome the land constraint and move into the Industrial Revolution as

110 A. C. L. Davies, *Perspectives on Labour Law* (Cambridge University Press, 2nd edn. 2009), at 4.

111 *Taff Vale Railway Co v Amalgamated Society of Railway Servants* [1901] AC 426 (HL), referred to in *idem*.

112 For a concise account see W. E. Forbath, *Law and the Shaping of the American Labor Movement* (Cambridge, Mass.: Harvard University Press, 1991).

113 See J. Pope, 'Worker Lawmaking, Sit-Down Strikes, and the Shaping of American Industrial Relations, 1935–1958' (2006) 24/1 *Law & History Review* 45.

114 See J. Pope, 'Contract, Race and Freedom of Labor in the Constitutional Law of 'Involuntary Servitude'' (2010) 119 *Yale Law Journal* 1474.

a result of slave-grown farm exports from plantations in the Caribbean, the Southern parts of the US and North-eastern Brazil.[115]

3.2.4 *Pollution and Third Parties*

The law-enabled asymmetry is also noticeable in the relations between producers and third parties affected by what we call today negative externalities, such as pollution. A number of historical studies[116] have shown that the legal framework introduced some oversight of industrial operations but that the thrust of the system was to provide a right of compensation to directly affected third parties, with no regard for the environment as such or future generations. The latter point seems natural, as concern for the environment and future generations did not arise until the second half of the XX century. However, it shows that the relevant laws took as their starting-point that industrial production could not have effects beyond contemporary humans (as noted by H. Jonas with respect to ethics) and, even among them, the prevailing approach was not to prevent, let alone block polluting activities, but to allow them subject to certain duties of compensation for their adverse impacts.

In an early contribution to the understanding of the (limited) role of nuisance law in the Industrial Revolution, J. Brenner argues that:

> the main explanation of the irrelevance of nuisance to industrialization lies not in the doctrine itself but rather in the fact that it was not applied precisely to those classes of parties who were most responsible for economic growth and pollution.[117]

More specifically, relying on the case law of mid XIX century England, Brenner shows that nuisance law was applied differently to individuals and factories, and hardly applied at all to quasi-public (chartered) enterprises, and that, in all events, there was no systematic prosecution of public nuisances. Even after the *Alkali Act* was adopted in 1863, placing the property of manufacturers under State oversight in order to protect the property of (large and wealthy) landowners,[118] the system of the Act soon became – and came to be seen – as a case of what today would be called regulatory capture, with very

115 Pomeranz, above n. 79, at 264. For a history of the Atlantic slave trade covering the relevant period see H. Thomas, *The Slave Trade: The Story of the Atlantic Slave Trade, 1440–1870* (New York: Simon & Schuster, 1997).

116 See above n. 92 the studies by Brenner (1974); Dingle (1982); Pontin (1998); Massard-Guilbaud (2010); Fressoz (2013).

117 Brenner, above n. 92, at 408; Dingle, above n. 92, at 537–538.

118 Dingle, above n. 92, at 529–530.

few prosecutions of alkali manufacturers.[119] In point of fact, manufacturers were generally favourable to the introduction of the *Alkali Act*, partly because they believed that cooperation would allow them to prevent more intrusive regulatory approaches such as the one followed in France, which dictated the location of a manufacture on the basis of its level of impact. Yet, even in France, the 1810 *Décret sur les établissements classés* was applied in a way that was highly accommodating for industrial activities[120] and the analysis of the private law case law of the time shows that the main approach was to compensate financially the damages suffered by third parties, and not to hinder industrial operations.[121]

Since the early days of the Industrial Revolution, legal controls over pollution have undergone fundamental changes, both from the perspective of regulatory oversight and private litigation. By and large, however, the conceptual underpinnings of the control systems are still shaped by the idea that production is to be organised first and then limitations added to deal with externalities. In other words, as noted earlier in this essay, environmental protection has still to become part of the DNA of law, including in those areas that organise production processes both domestically and internationally.

3.3 Asymmetric International Exchange Systems

3.3.1 *The British Atlantic System*

An important aspect in Pomeranz's explanation of the origins of the Industrial Revolution in England is, as already noted, reliance on raw materials from the Americas, Brazil and the Caribbean. Pomeranz shows that the purchase of English manufactures consumed most of the income received by these dependencies from the exports of sugar, corn or cotton, and that the labour for the production of such raw materials relied very heavily on slave trade.[122]

Trade had already become a concern of empire ideologists in the late XVII and early XVIII century.[123] David Armitage, a British historian, notes that by the mid XVIII century the Anglophone inhabitants of the British-shaped Atlantic world had started to describe their community (encompassing the UK, its Caribbean and North-American possessions, and to some extent African and the East Indies) as the 'British Empire'.[124] He quotes a contemporary writing

119 *Ibid*, at 545.
120 See generally Massard-Guilbaud (2010), above n. 92.
121 Fressoz, above n. 92, at 146.
122 See Pomeranz, above n. 79, chapter 6.
123 See D. Armitage, *The Ideological Origins of the British Empire* (Cambridge University Press, 2000), at 147–148.
124 *Ibid.*, at 171.

by Malachy Postlethwayt on *The African Trade, the Great Pillar and Support of the British Plantation Trade in America* (London, 1745), according to which: 'the General Navigation of Great Britain owes all its Encrease and Splendor to the Commerce of its American and African Colonies'.[125]

The domestic and international law of the time was instrumental in enabling the flows of slaves from Africa and the unequal exchange of manufactured goods from England against raw materials from the colonies and later the new world. Several aspects would have to be covered, including the lawfulness, until the early XIX century (and in some areas much later) of slavery, the laws regulating the freedom of the seas, and those organising market access and trade. In what follows, I briefly discuss the latter as it concerns the British Empire and the post-1945 world trade system.

3.3.2 *The Legal Organisation of Trade*

Initially, the approach pursued was a mercantilist one[126] shaped by the *Navigation Acts* of 1660, 1663, 1670 and 1673 whereby the trade relations of the British colonies were tightly regulated to prevent them from trading with other European powers – particularly the Dutch – and their colonies.[127] But as the industrial processes that characterised the Industrial Revolution unravelled, and the manufacturing sector's political influence grew stronger, a movement towards tariff reduction and free trade, first on a reciprocal basis and then unilaterally, gained ground in the UK. The analysis of the transition must necessarily be nuanced and integrate different levels,[128] including a diversity of political interests for and against trade liberalisation, the perceptions (whether justified or not empirically) of the advantages of free trade, and the international context. This movement culminated with the repeal of the *Corn Laws* in 1846 and later with a network of over fifty bilateral trade treaties

125 *Idem.*

126 *Ibid.*, at 166–167 (discussing the views of three influential analysts of trade, namely Josiah Child, Charles Davenant, and William Wood).

127 See G. M. Walton, 'The New Economic History and the Burdens of the Navigation Acts' (1971) 24/4 *Economic History Review* 533 (comparing three attempts at assessing the impact of the British trade system on the American colonies).

128 The repeal of the Corn Laws paving the way for British free trade policies has been described as a 'puzzle', which has not yet been adequately explained. See C. Schonhardt-Bailey, *From the Corn Laws to Free Trade: Interests, Ideas and Institutions in Historical Perspective* (Cambridge MA: MIT Press, 2006), at 1. The same author published a comprehensive four volume documentary history covering the XIX century: C. Schonhardt-Bailey (ed.), *The Rise of Free Trade* (London: Routledge, 1997).

that followed the conclusion of the Cobden-Chevalier treaty of 1860 between the UK and France.[129]

By the end of the XIX century, however, the market dominance on which the UK free trade approach relied for its expected success was challenged by a series of international developments, including highly protectionist policies in the US and Europe (e.g. France, Germany, Italy) shielding the agricultural and the industrial sector,[130] often to protect 'infant industries' that would later become major competitors of the UK's manufacturing sector. There has been significant debate as to whether the rise of protectionism in the late XIX century enabled growth in Europe and the Americas. The debate focuses mostly on explaining the observed positive correlation between trade protectionism and growth,[131] and it is of relevance to situate the evolution of international trade policy in the context of the two features of the Anthropocene highlighted in this essay, i.e. growth and inequality, and why law matters for them. The First World War and the inter-war period were characterised by extremely protectionist and opportunistic trade practices (so-called 'beggar-thy-neighbour' policies) centred on imperial blocks. Some explanations for the enactment of these policies in countries such as the UK, Germany and Japan (but not the US) point to the strong pressure from domestic manufacturers who faced increasing international competition and, unlike manufacturers in the US, had only small domestic markets to invest in major capacity enhancement.[132] Imperial protection offered a way of expanding the market while excluding competition.

The multilateral trade system established in the aftermath of the Second World War around the 1947 General Agreement on Tariffs and Trade (GATT)[133] and the failed International Trade Organisation (ITO)[134] sought to avoid precisely this type of inward policies, which were considered to have contributed to the outbreak of the war. But in establishing basic standards of trade

129 See M. Lampe, 'Explaining nineteenth-century bilateralism: economic and political determinants of the Cobden–Chevalier network' (2011) 64/2 *Economic History Review* 644 (explaining different drivers of the emergence of this treaty network).

130 See generally P. Bairoch (1989). 'European trade policy, 1815–1914.', in P. Mathias and S. Pollard (eds), *The Cambridge Economic History of Europe* (Cambridge University Press, 1989), vol. 8, at 1–160 (highlighting the link between protectionism and growth).

131 For an overview see K. H. O'Rourke, 'Tariffs and Growth in the Late 19th Century' (2000) 110 *The Economic Journal* 456.

132 See K. A. Chase, 'Imperial protection and strategic trade policy in the interwar period' (2004) 11/1 *Review of International Political Economy* 177.

133 General Agreement on Tariffs and Trade, 30 October 1947, 55 U.N.T.S. 194.

134 Havana Charter for an International Trade Organisation, 24 March 1948, UN Doc. E/Conf. 2178.

liberalisation across the board, such as the most-favoured-nation and national treatment clauses and the progressive reduction of trade tariffs through negotiation rounds, it also introduced a significant element of *de facto* inequality, as many countries could not compete in international trade markets. Interestingly, the very *de facto* discrimination (i.e. discrimination that results not from the face of the measure but from its actual application or the empirical conditions to which it applies) that the non-discrimination standards of the GATT seek to avoid among products is, to some extent, inherent to the general application of such standards to all countries, where very different initial conditions prevailed. Very soon, the *de facto* advantages provided by the world trade system to certain countries were challenged and several development countries together with a wave of newly independent countries emerging from the decolonisation process called for differential application of trade rules. These claims led to the creation of the United Nations Conference for International Trade and Development (UNCTAD) in 1964[135] to promote development matters in international trade negotiations.

However, the UNCTAD has faced great competition from other organisations focusing on growth and trade, such as the Organisation for Economic Co-operation and Development (OECD), which emerged from the post-war Marshall Plan, and above all the World Trade Organisation (WTO) established in 1994.[136] Matters of inequality remain prominent in the more recent green industrial policies required to effect the transition to a low carbon economy.[137] Protectionist policies, even when they seek the protection of an environmental infant industry (e.g. renewable energy) have been challenged as breaches of non-discrimination standards (see section 5.3.3 below). It is no exaggeration to say that, under current trade rules, environmental protection measures can be lawfully adopted only to the extent that they are consistent with trade liberalisation.[138]

Viewed from the perspective of the Anthropocene narrative, this conclusion amounts to a confirmation of what was suggested earlier in this essay, namely that legal institutions are built in such a way that socio-economic growth/development is organised first and only then environmental protection concerns are added, as external and additional. More fundamentally, the growth/

135 See United Nations Conference for Trade and Development, *UNCTAD at 50: A Short History* (Geneva: United Nations, 2014).

136 Agreement establishing the World Trade Organisation, 15 April 1994, 1867 U.N.T.S. 154.

137 See e.g. United Nations Environment Programme/International Institute for Sustainable Development, *Trade and the Green Economy. A Handbook* (third edn. 2014), at 1.

138 See P.-M. Dupuy, J. E. Viñuales, *International Environmental Law* (Cambridge University Press, 2015), at 400.

development system entrenched in legal institutions favours those countries that were already competitive when the new standards came into play, and they may become means to thwart or delay transition to a new socio-technical regime. In short, the inequalities in the production processes and prosperity that have led to the Anthropocene can also be read in past and existing legal institutions.

3.4 Operationalising Historical Responsibility

3.4.1 *Level and Time-Horizon*

An important question is whether law can reflect the different historical inequalities and responsibilities of different human groups for the advent of the Anthropocene and, if so, through which means and approaches. As with previous questions, the range of legal concepts potentially relevant is wide. They include the bodies of law specifically developed to allocate responsibility for environmental action (e.g. allocation of regulatory responsibility)[139] and damage (responsibility/liability/compensation)[140] but also those governing access to justice[141] and the organisation of redress processes,[142] and even foundational concepts such as those of legal personality, representation, obligation, debt, causality or damage.

In order to provide a meaningful structure to the inquiry, two analytical clarifications appear useful. Firstly, although the reference to historical responsibility does not necessarily exclude individual liability or individual damage, I will situate my inquiry at a broader level capable of reflecting the magnitude entailed in the term 'historical'. I do not mean that an individual's action or his/her suffering may never reach historical proportions, as Hitler's monstrous decision to trigger a genocide or, conversely, Mandela's heroic decision to peacefully tolerate long years of prison certainly did. But the concepts capable of reflecting the historical responsibility for the Anthropocene would

139 For an example of this broad question in a specific regulatory context see J. van Zeben, *The Allocation of Regulatory Competence in the EU Emissions Trading Scheme* (Cambridge University Press, 2014).

140 For a comparative study see M. Hinteregger (ed.), *Environmental Liability and Ecological Damage in European Law* (Cambridge University Press, 2008).

141 See the seminal study by C. Stone, 'Should Trees have Standing? Towards Legal Rights for Natural Objects' (1972) 45 *California Law Review* 450.

142 For two studies focusing on different areas of redress see P. de Greif (ed.), *The Handbook of Reparations* (Oxford University Press, 2008); H. Holtzmann, E. Kristjánsdóttir (eds.), *International Mass Claims Processes* (Oxford University Press, 2007).

have to refer to the action or suffering of more aggregate entities, such as future generations, or slaves, or oppressed peoples, or small island nations, or certain non-human species. Secondly, the time direction implicit in legal approaches is also important. Some of them (e.g. historical debt or mass redress mechanisms) look mainly at the past, whereas some others (e.g. representation of future generations) are more forward-looking. Between the two, the allocation of responsibility for action among contemporaneous actors provides a basis to organise present action (whether such action is mainly backward- or forward-looking).

With these two clarifications in mind, the purpose of this section is to survey three ways of fleshing out legally the historical responsibilities arising from the advent of the Anthropocene, namely historical redress processes (3.4.2), the legal recognition of future generations (3.4.3), and the allocation of responsibility for present action (3.4.4).

3.4.2 *Industrialisation and the Historical Debt towards Africans*

I have already mentioned the important advantage offered by the slave trade in the advent of the Industrial Revolution in England at the beginning of the XIX century. The same considerations could be extended to native peoples in the Americas as well as to other oppressed groups, whose labour and resources were instrumental in the economic equation that, according to Pomeranz, enabled the Industrial Revolution. From a legal perspective, two main approaches have been followed to address such past injustices. One concerns the normative concepts grounding the need for redress, such as the concepts of 'debt', 'responsibility' or 'obligation'. The other focuses on the actual redress mechanisms, whether in the context of mass property claims or transitional justice. Unsurprisingly, the operational nature of the second approach makes it relatively more effective (albeit often controversial and highly criticised) than the first approach. Yet, redress mechanisms would normally rely on a prior allocation of responsibility. Depending on the circumstances of the case, such allocation is softened by a variety of 'restorative justice' tools that seek to make up for the victims suffering without incriminating – or not fully – their victimisers, at least when the latter still wield sufficient power to interfere with the transition.

The close connection between the concepts used to translate injustice into responsibility and the redress mechanisms that may be used at an operational level can be illustrated by reference to a debate concerning the historical responsibility of the West for the African slave trade. In a special issue of the journal *African Studies Quarterly*, a number of contributions addressed redress options ranging from the creation of a tribunal[143] (based on the idea of criminal responsibility) to compensation for the African contribution to the development of Europe[144] (based on considerations akin to unjust enrichment) to the development of an African Marshall Plan[145] (relying on a restorative – rather than punitive – justice approach). Of particular interest is A. Mazrui's contribution, which is based on an earlier and more developed study published in 1994 in the *African Studies Review* and based on his inaugural Bashroun M. K. O. Abiola Distinguished Lecture.[146] Writing in the context of what he saw as the emerging 'Reparationist' movement, fostered by a resolution adopted by the Organisation of African Unity (O.A.U.) in 1993 and calling for the compensation of a 'unique and unprecedented moral debt owed to the African peoples which has yet to be paid',[147] Mazrui asks whether 'the restitution [should] be calculated on the basis of the pain of the slave or the profit of the slaver'.[148] He reasons that both have to be taken into account and refers, specifically, to the 'era of the labor imperative [...] when the West was interested primarily in African labor – and was prepared to promote slave raids, the Middle Passage and slave plantations to ensure that kind of exploitation of African labor.'[149] Referring to this era, Mazrui's 1999 article expounds the same relation between slave trade and the Industrial Revolution as the one discussed by Pomeranz, whereby:

> labor of Africa's sons and daughters was what the West needed for its industrial take-off. The slave ship helped to export millions to the Americas to help in the agrarian revolution in the Americas and the industrial revolution in Europe simultaneously.[150]

---

143 Ricardo Laremont, 'Political versus Legal Strategies for the African Slavery Reparations Movement' (1999) 2/4 *African Studies Quarterly* 13.

144 Ali Mazrui, 'From Slave Ship to Space Ship: Africa between Marginalization and Globalization' (1999) 2/4 *African Studies Quarterly* 5.

145 D. Thomson, 'The Debt Has Not Been Paid, the Accounts Have Not Been Settled' (1999) 2/4 *African Studies Quarterly* 19 (Thomson derives the idea of a Marshall plan for Africa from previous proposals, including from Mazrui).

146 A. Mazrui, 'Global Africa: From Abolitionists to Reparationists' (1994) 37/3 *African Studies Review* 1.

147 'The Abuja Proclamation', Declaration of the first Abuja Pan-African Conference on Reparations for African Enslavement, Colonization and Neo-Colonization, sponsored by The Organization of African Unity and its Reparations Commission, April 27–29, 1993, Abuja, Nigeria.

148 Mazrui, above n. 146, at 8.

149 *Ibid.*, at 9 (referring to J. H. Clarke's *African People in World History*, Baltimore: Black Classic Press, 1993, at 51–71).

150 Mazrui, above n. 144, at 5.

This is not the only basis Mazrui sees for reparation, as the imperialist powers also benefited from African lands and natural resources, but the key consideration here is that the historical debt rests both on historical/ongoing damage to Africa and on a form of unjust enrichment, the extreme form of which was the economic compensation received by slavers for the emancipation of slaves. The redress mechanisms would have to reflect these different bases and involve not only monetary transfers but also empowerment strategies of Africans with respect to their own State machines as well as with respect to the World.

One specific attempt at claiming such reparation was made in the conclusions of the African World Reparation and Repatriation Truth Commission that met in Accra, Ghana, in August 1999 and asked 'the West' to pay 777 trillion to Africa within a period of five years as reparation for the slave trade.[151] This initiative, influenced by the transitional process undertaken in South Africa at the end of the apartheid regime as well as by other redress processes (including reparations paid to Jewish victims of Nazism, native Americans, and other groups), reflected only the loss of life and the value of resources looted during the period of British rule.[152] Significantly, the scope of the debt relevant from the perspective of the Anthropocene narrative is not merely the resource debt or even the ecological degradation of the land,[153] but more generally the enslavement of large portions of a continent to sustain a production system that has led to the Anthropocene. The narrow confines of environmental law or the measuring of environmental degradation would be utterly insufficient to capture this broader debt.

3.4.3 *The Legal Representation of Future Generations*

The time-horizon of the debt and associated redress mechanisms is particularly important in the Anthropocene narrative not only retrospectively (as discussed in the previous section) but also prospectively to the extent that our generation and the preceding ones will be leaving a more challenging Earth system to future generations. From a normative standpoint, the need to provide protection to future generations has received ample attention in the last decades. Of particular note is the work of Edith Brown Weiss on the

151 J. Fast, *Beyond Bullying: Breaking the Cycle of Shame, Bullying and Violence* (Oxford University Press, 2016), at 199.

152 *Idem.*

153 See Mazrui, above n. 146, at 9 (referring to the role of ecological degradation in preventing the socio-economic development of Africa).

legal dimensions of the principle of intergenerational equity.[154] This principle, which has been formulated in a number of constitutional[155] and international instruments,[156] aims to balance the interests of present generations with those of future generations as regards development and environmental protection, but it can also have a procedural dimension.[157]

A significant problem in fleshing out the protection of future generations is whether they are to be deemed a subject[158] with its own interests and capacity to act (through representation) or a mere object to be directly (as such) or indirectly (through the protection of the environment as such) protected. The choice between these different approaches has important institutional implications, particularly as regards the degree of agency to be provided to future generations (as acting subjects rather than objects). A 2013 report prepared by the UN Secretary-General[159] following a recommendation from the outcome document of the 2012 Rio Summit on Sustainable Development[160] identified a number of institutional options to give a voice to future generations, essentially in the form of representation through commissioners or other agents. The report stands out, as a document arising from the UN bureaucracy, for the attention paid to theoretical questions. It devotes several pages to the theoretical foundations of intergenerational equity, reviewing several statements and instruments that acknowledge the need for some degree of solidarity with and representation of future generations. It then moves to a review of institutional developments at the international and domestic levels.

---

154 E. Brown Weiss, *In Fairness to Future Generations: International Law, Common Patrimony and Intergenerational Equity* (United Nations University, 1989).

155 See J. C. Tremmel, 'Establishing intergenerational justice in national constitutions', in J. C. Tremmel (ed.), *Handbook of Intergenerational Justice* (Cheltenham: Edward Elgar, 2006), at 187–216.

156 See C. Molinari, 'Principle 3: From a Right to Development to Intergenerational Equity', in J. E. Viñuales (ed.), *The Rio Declaration on Environment and Development. A Commentary* (Oxford University Press, 2015), at 139–156.

157 See e.g. *Minors Oposa v. Secretary of the Department of Environment and Natural Resources* (DENR)(1994) 33 ILM 173 (30 July 1993), 185 (where the Philippines Supreme Court granted *jus standi* to future generations on the basis of the principle of intergenerational equity in the Constitution of the Philippines); *State of Himachal Pradesh and others v. Ganesh Wood Products and others*, 1995 (6) SCC 363 (where an Indian court took the principle of intergenerational equity into account in assessing the legality of the granting of a permit), cited in Ramlogan, R., *Sustainable Development: Towards a Judicial Interpretation* (Leiden: Martinus Nijhoff, 2011) 226.

158 See e.g. *E. H. P. v. Canada*, HRC Complaint no. 67/1980 (27 October 1982), para 8(a) (where the Human Rights Committee considered a reference made by the applicants to future generations as a mere way of expressing additional concern).

159 UN Secretary-General, *Intergenerational Solidarity and the Needs of Future Generations. Report of the Secretary-General*, 15 August 2013, UN Doc A/68/322.

160 *Ibid.*, para 86.

The report reviews developments in Canada, Finland, Hungary, Israel, New Zealand and Wales, where specific committees, commissions or commissioners were established starting in the 1980s to protect the environment, including – sometimes explicitly – the rights of future generations. The first specific Commission for future generations was established in Israel in 2001 and the position of Commissioner was held by a judge, Shlomo Shoham.[161] Although the Commission was disbanded in 2007, it is worth recalling the type of tasks that were entrusted to this institution. The Commission had both investigative and advisory functions. It could seek information from different agencies regarding the implications of acts and pieces of legislation for future generations and make recommendations to the Parliament. A more advanced institutional approach was later created in Hungary, where the Parliamentary Commissioner for Future Generations, *Sándor Fülöp,* was tasked with the protection of the constitutional right to a healthy environment and, to this effect, he could also hear individual complaints from affected citizens.[162] The role of the Hungarian Commissioner was that of an ombudsman, although it also had investigative and advisory powers, including that of advocating legislation promoting the rights of future generations. The function was later subsumed under a single overall role of Commissioner for Fundamental Rights, but one of the Commissioner's deputies, Marcel Szabó, kept the specific task of advancing the interests of future generations. A third illustration is provided by the Commissioner for Sustainable Futures, a position created by the Welsh government in 2011 and later transformed, on a specific statutory basis (the *Well-being of Future Generations Act* of 2015), into a Future Generations Commissioner. Unlike the previous examples, the Commissioners who have subsequently held these positions, Peter Davies and Sophie Howe, have essentially an advisory role although they can take a wide range of initiatives to promote sustainable development.

At present, there have been calls for extending the representation of future generations through the creation of a similar 'guardian' position at the level of the European Union.[163] Some of the deficiencies that such an institution would address include the insufficient reflection of the interests of future generations

161 For an assessment see S. Shoham, N. Lamay, 'Commission for future generations in the Knesset: Lessons learnt', in J. C. Tremmel (ed.), *Handbook of Intergenerational Justice* (Cheltenham: Edward Elgar, 2006), at 244–281.

162 For an assessment see E. T. Ambrusné, 'The Parliamentary Commissioner for Future Generations of Hungary and his impact' (2010) 10/1 *Intergenerational Justice Review* 18.

163 See M. Nesbit, A. Illés, *Establishing an EU 'Guardian for Future Generations', Report and recommendations for the World Future Council* (London: Institute for European Environmental Policy, 2015).

in the choice of discount factors within cost-benefit analysis assessments[164] or in the policies relating to areas such as climate change or nuclear energy.[165]

3.4.4 *Present Allocations: Common but Differentiated Responsibilities*

The allocation of the benefits and burden of protecting the environment among present generations has been fleshed out through the concept of differentiation[166] and a number of more specific expressions, such as the principle of common but differentiated responsibilities (CBDR).[167] The latter has played a prominent role in the negotiations concerning global environmental problems, such as climate change and biodiversity, but also the protection of the ozone layer or the control of persistent organic pollutants. Although broadly accepted as a principle, the specific implications of CBDR are controversial in many ways as, depending on its interpretation, it can result in very different allocations of responsibility. A comparison of how the principle has been fleshed out in three treaty contexts will help illustrate this point.

The first clear (albeit implicit) expression of the principle of CBDR is the 1987 Montreal Protocol on Substances that Deplete the Ozone Layer.[168] The 'common' and 'differentiated' aspects of the responsibility for the protection of the ozone layer are articulated through a distinction between core production/consumption obligations, which are common to developed and developing countries alike (the latter are called parties 'operating under Article 5'), and the modalities of implementation, which are more lenient for developing countries (which are given more time to phase out the relevant substances and can benefit from financial and technological assistance). A different approach has been followed by the Kyoto Protocol to the UNFCCC,[169] under which only developed countries and countries in transition to a market economy (Annex B) have quantified emission reduction obligations (Article 3 and Annex B) whereas developing countries, including many of the main emitters of greenhouse gases, such as China, are not subject to any new obligations

164 *Ibid.*, at 15–17.

165 *Ibid.*, at 17–18.

166 See M. Hébié, 'Principle 6: Special Situation of Developing Countries', in J. E. Viñuales (ed.), *The Rio Declaration on Environment and Development. A Commentary* (Oxford University Press, 2015), at 207–228.

167 See P. Cullet, 'Principle 7: Common but Differentiated Responsibilities', in J. E. Viñuales (ed.), *The Rio Declaration on Environment and Development. A Commentary* (Oxford University Press, 2015), at 229–244.

168 Montreal Protocol on Substances that Deplete the Ozone Layer, 16 September 1987, 1522 UNTS 29, art. 5.

169 Kyoto Protocol to the UN Framework Convention on Climate Change, 11 December 1997, 2303 UNTS 148.

under the protocol (Article 10). This so-called 'Chinese wall' between developed and developing countries reflected the historical emissions argument according to which developed countries, by virtue of their early industrialisation, have mostly caused the carbon budget of the troposphere to be overused.[170] In such a legal architecture, the differentiated aspects of the CBDR principle have clearly prevailed over the common ones.

However, the trends in emissions and emitters since the early 1990s have significantly changed, with many developing countries now appearing as the main present and future emitters. In order to bring these countries under some form of mitigation discipline, the process leading to the adoption of the Paris Agreement on climate change in December 2015[171] had to resort to a different way of fleshing out the CBDR principle. The key difference lies in the fact that, instead of focusing on a plethora of criteria or formulae for differentiation among States, as the mainstream literature suggested, differentiation was effected at the level of the very objects to be distributed (e.g. burden of emission reductions, financial contributions, access to different forms of assistance, etc.) each with its own distribution key.[172] For mitigation, the overall system established by the Agreement is similar to all States and is based on unilateral declarations by each State of its own targets (called 'nationally determined contribution' or NDC) and long-term low carbon strategies, to be revised up at regular intervals of time (Article 4). The unilateral character of such declarations allows countries to specifically tailor the contents of such declaration to their circumstances and plans. In addition, developing countries are to receive financial (Article 9), technological (Article 10) and capacity-building support (Article 11) from developed countries and potentially from other countries as well (e.g. emerging economies) to realise their targets under the Agreement. The overall system is one in which more leeway is granted to those countries that did not participate in the early stages of the Industrial Revolution and

170 The Subsidiary Body for Scientific and Technological Advice (SBSTA) under the UNFCCC undertook a programme to flesh out methodologically the CBDR principle (called 'MATCH'), except for questions of land use change. See N. Höhne et al., *Summary report of the ad- hoc group for the modelling and assessment of contributions to climate change (MATCH) (2008)*, available at: www.unfccc.int.

171 'Adoption of the Paris Agreement', Decision 1/CP.21, 12 December 2015, FCCC/CP/2015/L.9, Annex (Paris Agreement).

172 For an early exposition of this approach see J. E. Viñuales, 'Balancing Effectiveness and Fairness in the Re-design of the Climate Change Regime' (2011) 24/1 *Leiden Journal of International Law* 223. On the use of this approach in the Paris Agreement, see L. Rajamani, 'Ambition and Differentiation in the 2015 Paris Agreement: Interpretative Possibilities and Underlying Politics' (2016) 65/2 *International and Comparative Law Quarterly* 493.

whose current developmental priorities are seen as a justification for a higher environmental footprint.

The inequalities expressly consented by differentiation systems are important to reflect inequalities in responsibilities and impact in the past as well as respective capabilities. However, redressing inequalities may have unintended effects which are particularly clear in the climate change context to the extent that there are limits in the amount of greenhouse gases that may be emitted if the problem is to be tackled. Integrating both effectiveness and equity in our response to the Anthropocene challenge is a daunting enterprise from both a political and an operational perspective. As discussed next, law has an important role to play in this regard, as it can organise not only the response but also the processes through which such a response is to be considered legitimate.

Part 4: Legal Organisation of the Transition

1 *Preliminary Observations*

For as far as there are reliable written records, law has been widely used to organise and contain the consequences of the major shifts in power and wealth entailed by transitional processes.[173] A transition of the magnitude required to manage our newly acquired powers with their deleterious effects on the Earth system will certainly entail major shifts. In point of fact, what we face as a species, with unequal responsibilities, is a series of transition processes closely but often unclearly interrelated. Whether one thinks of the climate-driven transition from a fossil to a low-carbon energy matrix or of the climate/population/pollution-driven transformation of agricultural and food production systems or, still, of the move from a waste disposal to a circular reuse system, the institutional and operational changes that will need to be phased-in and those that will be phased-out are of gargantuan dimensions.

To situate the role of law in managing this transition, it is first necessary to clarify our very understanding of these processes as 'transitions'. The use of

173 After the restoration of democracy in Athens in 403 B.C., a complex legal system was used to manage the transition, particularly as regards amnesty for crimes committed during the dictatorship and oligarchic periods and the restitution of property. On these two points see, respectively: D. Cohen, 'The rhetoric of justice: strategies of reconciliation and revenge in the restoration of Athenian democracy in 403 BC' (2001) 42/2 *Archives européennes de sociologie* 335, at 338; J. Elster, *Closing the Books: Transition Justice in Historical Perspective* (Cambridge University Press, 2004), at 13. For a specific study of this transition see T. C. Loening, *The Reconciliation Agreement of 403/402 B.C. in Athens* (Stuttgard: Franz Steiner Verlag, 1987).

the term transition in this context is not innocuous[174] as it deliberately seeks to play down the existence of a 'crisis' and suggests a certain incrementality or progressiveness of the process rather than an abrupt change. In addition, the term transition conveys the idea of a 'managed' process, which in turn calls for an elucidation of both the techniques used to manage it and the source of legitimacy of the 'manager' driving and accompanying the process. In introducing the implications of the term transition as well as its deliberate and reflexive character, I will seek to lay the wider humanities/social science foundations of the specific questions that law is capable of answering. As before, the main reason for the detour is to integrate the legal inquiry conducted in this essay to the much wider research agenda relating to the Anthropocene.

2 *The Transitional Narrative in Energy Studies*

The prevailing understanding of the evolution of energy systems holds that there have been phases dominated respectively by animal/human strength, wind and water mills, wood, coal and oil as the main energy resource, punctuated by phase transitions from one era to the other.[175] In addition, starting in the 1950s and 1960s, there was some expectation that nuclear energy would be the next leader, although this forecast never fully materialised. Instead, the energy matrix remained dominated by the use of fossil fuels, with important additions from nuclear and hydroelectric energy and, much more recently, other renewable sources such as solar, wind and biomass (including, ironically, wood). In order to understand the implications of the transitional narrative, one must first look at the discourse that gradually introduced it. Although there is no comprehensive literature review that could serve as a basis for this task, some partial attempts at looking at the relevant data and theoretical sources have been published over time. Here, I will focus on one recent review, which is both comprehensive and balanced.[176] It must also be noted that the transitional narrative appears in some of the main historiographical accounts of the role of energy in the Industrial Revolution[177] as well as energy history

174 Bonneuil/Fressoz, above n. 1, at 121–122.

175 For a concise long-term account see V. Smil, 'World History and Energy' (2004) *Encyclopedia of Energy* vol. 1, at 549–561.

176 A. Grubler, 'Energy transitions research: Insights and cautionary tales' (2012) 50 *Energy Policy* 8.

177 D. S. Landes, *The Unbound Prometheus. Technological Change and Industrial Development in Western Europe from 1750 to the Present* (Cambridge University Press, 2nd edn 2003 [1969]) (Landes characterises the Industrial Revolution as a succession of technological changes, particularly the rise of the steam engine, but also new forms of industrial organisation, particularly the 'factory system').

tout court.[178] After briefly reviewing this body of literature and, indeed, of conceptualisation of our understanding of energy as a social process, I will turn to the relevance of this debate for our more specific legal inquiry.

The transitional narrative has been widely endorsed to make sense of trajectories that initially appeared as data, mostly of energy supply but, increasingly, also of energy demand (end use). In other words, and perhaps unsurprisingly, statistical energy data came first and interpretation and theory, in the form of transitional theories, came later.[179] In curves depicting the relative share of each energy source over time (i.e. the percentage of each source in the overall energy matrix[180]), changes from one source to the other appear as transitions. Moreover, for early adopters, the rise of new energy sources was a long and slow process spanning, for the modern transitions, approximately 130 years (for the phasing in of coal and steam power in the Industrial Revolution) and 80 years (for the phasing in of oil, gas and electricity).[181] There is a body of literature suggesting that for late adopters (countries, political units, companies, etc.) the pace of the transition can be much faster as it relies on the experience gained by early adopters.[182] A. Grubler summarises this point, by reference to the phasing in and out of coal and steam, with the simple expression 'first in,

178 V. Smil, *Energy in World History* (Boulder CO: Westview Press, 1994) (Smil's study is a major effort to defeat deterministic accounts of energy's role in world history. He considers critically the tendency of such grand accounts of energy and human history to identify energy eras and energy transitions. His analysis highlights, however, the dominant role of such accounts in understanding the history of energy use).

179 Grubler, above n. 176, at 9 (referring to some pioneering efforts to gather and refine data on energy at the international level – from P. C. Putnam, *Energy in the Future* (New York: Van Nostrand, 1953) to A. Kander et al., *Power to the People. Energy in Europe over the Last Five Centuries* (Princeton NJ: Princeton University Press, 2012) – or at the domestic level – e.g. S. H. Schurr, B. C. Netschert, *Energy in the American Economy 1850–1975* (Baltimore: John Hopkins Press, 1960) or R. Fouquet, P. J. G. Pearson, 'A thousand years of energy use in the United Kingdom' (1998) 19/4 *The Energy Journal* 1).

180 Bonneuil and Fressoz rightly caution against conflating this relative measure of the role of a given energy source (e.g. coal accounting for more than 60% of the energy sources used at time 1) with absolute measures (e.g. if the energy consumption at time 2 is three times as large as that at time 1, even if coal accounts for 30% of the new energy matrix, much more coal is being consumed in absolute terms at time 2 than at time 1). They hold this confusion as a major problem presented by accounts of energy transitions, which, in their view, obscure the levels of overall consumption. See Bonneuil/Fressoz, above n. 1.

181 Grubler, above n. 176, at 11–12.

182 See M. Frankel, 'Obsolescence and technological change in a maturing economy' (1955) 45(3) *American Economic Review* 296; A. Grubler, 'Time for a change: On the patterns of diffusion of innovation' (1996) 125/3 *Daedalus* 19; B. Gales et al., 'North versus south: energy transitions and energy intensity in Europe over 200 years' (2006) 11/2 *European Review of Economic History* 219; C. Wilson, *Meta-analysis of Unit and Industry Level Scaling*

last out; last in, first out'.[183] Thus, the UK and Germany were early adopters of coal and steam (as compared to late adopters such as Italy and Sweden) and they phased out this energy matrix later than late adopters.[184] Another important way in which this literature relies on the concept of transitions is by identifying sequential stages in the development and diffusion of energy technologies, starting with a long but critical period of experimentation and learning at the technology units level (e.g. engine, turbine, nuclear reactor, solar panel), which are then scaled up in order to benefit from economies of scale (e.g. larger units), which subsequently turn into a major industry servicing core markets and, eventually, move from core markets to other (rim and peripheral) markets through trade and investment.[185] Significantly, this body of research suggests that the stages in the up-scaling process are sequential and not simultaneous, which further anchors the idea of transitional processes.

Moreover, a combination of empirical studies and more specific theoretical models[186] suggests that the role of policy in the emergence and, even more, the refinement and diffusion of technologies is of particular importance. For present purposes, three insights must be highlighted. Firstly, as already mentioned, empirical studies show that the initial phase of emergence, experimentation and refinement is critical for the up-scaling of new technologies.[187] Secondly, also from an empirical perspective, it has been widely shown that new technologies have to face 'socio-technical regimes' that are deeply grounded (both in terms of sunk investments but also rules – laws – and power relations) on existing technologies.[188] Thirdly, the up-scaling and diffusion process is a competitive and often confrontational one where the established participants in the regime incur higher costs (scrapping infrastructure and investment) and potentially decline in moving into a new socio-technical regime (as suggested by the 'first in, last out' insight), and they are likely to use the means at their disposal to prevent the change or at least to make it less costly and gain time.

Dynamics in Energy Technologies and Climate Change Mitigation Scenarios, IR-09-029 (Laxenburg: International Institute for Applied Systems Analysis, 2009).

183 Grubler, above n. 176, at 12.

184 *Ibid.*, at 13 (figure 2).

185 *Ibid.*, at 14 (discussing the work of C. Wilson, above n. 182).

186 F. Geels, 'The multi-level perspective in sustainability transitions: Response to seven criticisms' (2011) 1 *Environmental Innovation and Societal Transitions* 24 (discussing and addressing recurrent criticisms of the multi-level perspective (MLP) of socio-technical transitions and offering a useful literature review).

187 See Wilson, above n. 182.

188 Geels, above n. 186, at 27–28 (characterizing the concept and referring to the literature on applications of the MLP to transitions of electricity systems, transportation systems or biogas, among others).

Such trade-offs between industries also involve trade-offs between individuals (e.g. workers in the old model may lose their jobs) and countries (e.g. countries deeply invested in the old technology may lose ground to new entrants) and, above all, values (e.g. reducing unemployment and offering cheap electricity versus protecting health from air pollution or mitigating climate change). For example, fighting climate change may entail for some emerging economies the need to move massively into renewable energy generation. From the perspective of energy transition theory, such a move by latecomers makes much sense as it entails lower levels of investment scrapping and can accelerate the adoption of the new technology, with the ensuing mitigation effects benefitting all countries. However, it also challenges an established regime (entrenched, among others, in international trade, investment and intellectual property rules) with its own beneficiaries. As discussed next, these three aspects of transitions are of particular relevance from a legal perspective.

3 *Law and Sustainability Transitions*

3.1 Overview

As discussed in the preceding section, technological transitions and, more generally, sustainability transitions call for policy (and hence legal) change. When such policy changes are attempted or introduced, different legal means may be used to either promote (e.g. new patents) or to hinder (e.g. patent infringement litigation) such developments. In addition, beyond the pragmatic aspects of promoting/hindering change, law plays a critical role in offering avenues to legitimising change.

These three aspects of the legal organisation of transitions, namely the legal form of policy changes, the legal means to promote or hinder such changes, and the wider legal frameworks capable of legitimising them, all call for further elucidation. As in previous sections, the field is too vast to be covered even superficially within the confines of this essay. My purpose is only to frame the broad legal questions that would have to be addressed and, when possible, to discuss the most relevant legal literature. To better understand the nature of these three inquiries, it may be useful to recall a distinction made by A. Supiot in the context of his critique of labour law,[189] namely the one between a conception of norms and regulation as technical fine-tuning or optimisation, and another conception according to which norms express moral choices.

The first inquiry discussed next (3.2) is clearly based on the optimisation conception, where law is seen as a technology conveying pre-determined

189 Supiot, above n. 91, at X–XIII.

scientific truths (rather than fundamental normative choices) and, as a result, the objective of legal research is to make the instrument (law and regulation) fit for purpose. At the other end, the third inquiry (3.4) is based on the assumption that social choices cannot be fully pre-determined by scientific truths and, therefore, an explicit normative or value choice is an indispensable and unavoidable step in policy- and decision-making. The fact that law may be mostly, but never entirely, the expression of one of these two conceptions is well illustrated by the second aforementioned inquiry, namely that focusing on how law may promote or hinder policy change (3.3).

3.2 Adaptive Legal Systems

Law, when considered as a regulative instrument, becomes a technology that can be fine-tuned and optimised to reach a stated purpose. Some of the work that has been done to explore the role of law in the Anthropocene follows this perspective and argues in favour of a regulatory paradigm where law would become an 'adaptive system'.[190]

In a collection of works edited by A. S. Garmestani and C. R. Allen, several case-studies relating to wildlife and biodiversity protection, natural preserves, marine protected areas, water governance and climate change are discussed from the perspective of socio-ecological resilience, characterised as a change within the system rather than of the system (regime change).[191] The goal of the book is to contribute to the design of legal systems that are capable of remaining relevant (regulative) even in cases of regime change. As discussed previously in this essay, the wide assumption on which law-making processes are based is that nature does not fundamentally change or, as the contributors to that volume note, that 'the environment, ecosystems, and natural resources are presumed to exist in a particular condition or state'.[192] Once that state is defined, the conventional approach to environmental regulation is to introduce a legal framework to keep the system in that state, for example, by limiting extraneous inputs or interference (e.g. pollutants) within limits that allow the system to return to its equilibrium. However, socio-ecological systems cannot be conceptualised as having a single equilibrium. Rather, there is substantial evidence suggesting that ecosystems can exist in a variety of stable states. In order to adapt to the constant change in socio-ecological systems, laws and regulations

---

190 See Garmestani/Allen, above n. 14; Baker, above n. 16.

191 Garmestani/Allen, above n. 14, at 6 (defining socio-ecological resilience as 'the amount of disturbance a linked socio-ecological system can absorb before reorganizing into a state characterized by a different set of processes and structures').

192 *Ibid.*, at 2.

must be managed as adaptive systems that try different types of interventions on the basis of different understandings of a problem and adjust accordingly as the results of such interventions are known. The authors acknowledge the need for law to provide a certain degree of certainty, hence of rigidity, and the ability of law to adapt to changing human values, but they argue that such an approach to regulation remains inadequate for ecological processes and features:

> The maladaptive nature of law can allow, facilitate, or even mandate pathological choices and behaviors with respect to ecosystems. It can contribute to incidents of ecological collapse, which in turn lead to incidents of social collapse.[193]

Different legal techniques inspired on adaptive management (e.g. more flexible legal interventions capable of being adjusted on the basis of the feedback received from the monitoring of their impact) could be used to fine-tune legal systems, and the contributors to the volume discuss some of them with emphasis on the administrative and environmental law of the United States.

The detail of these techniques is less important for present purposes than the overall approach expounded by the editors and contributors of the volume, which is genuinely regulative in that it seeks to optimise the ability of legal systems with respect to socio-ecological processes. Degradation of ecological processes can indeed lead to collapse of social processes, but excessive protection of the environment may also have adverse social effects. The great uncertainties entailed by these complex interactions hence call for a constant adjustment and fine-tuning of the regulatory system. Interestingly, the process of fine-tuning seeks some form of scientific optimality but it displays limited sensitivity to other features of real life, such as the dynamics of socio-technical transitions, politics, vested interests, and also the need for legal certainty or of a strong signal to guide new investment, with which law must also cope. More fundamentally, this approach focuses on the legal frameworks facing environmental problems or, in other words, those addressing externalities, and it tends to overemphasise the rigidity of such frameworks. What is missing is a much broader understanding of legal concepts whereby it is not only the protective or regulative system that is fine-tuned but also the organisation of the transactions that cause the negative externalities (e.g. the legal form of business organisations) and even the foundational legal categories structuring such systems (e.g. causality in the attribution of liability for environmental harm).

193 *Ibid.*, at 5.

Even if law is envisaged mostly as a technology, the underpinnings of the technology are much broader than the sole environmental law or the laws dealing directly with environmental problems.

3.3 Promoting or Hindering the Transition

Law plays a major role in signalling and prompting or, conversely, preventing social change. The analysis of sustainability transitions cannot overlook this dimension. Yet, technology-focused models rarely pay any attention to the legal form of recommended policy interventions,[194] even when they explicitly aim to cover rules and institutions.[195] This is problematic because legal form does matter, as can be illustrated from a current example.

The recent conclusion of the Paris Agreement on Climate Change[196] was largely facilitated by an initial understanding between the two main emitters of greenhouse gases, China and the United States. A key part of this understanding was the effort of the US administration to regulate emissions from power plants through the so-called 'Clean Power Plan' (CPP), a regulation from the US Environmental Protection Agency, published in late 2015.[197] The adoption of a concrete measure to tackle its main source of emissions made the US' commitment to a climate deal credible to the eyes of both China and the rest of the world. However, such action rests on potentially fragile legal grounds. Although the Obama administration initially sought to have a specific Act (the 'Clean Energy and Security Act' or 'Waxman-Markey Bill') passed through the US Congress, that option was not politically viable due to opposition in the Senate. The administration then turned to another avenue, a legal enabler, namely using the authority already delegated by Congress to it in a piece of legislation several decades old, the *Clean Air Act* (CAA), which authorises regulation to fight air pollution.[198] Through an earlier reinterpretation

194 New and more realistic modeling approaches may be capable of addressing this deficiency, see J.-F. Mercure et al., 'Modelling complex systems of heterogeneous agents to better design sustainability transitions policy', (2016) 37 *Global Environmental Change* 102.

195 As in the case of the multi-level perspective of socio-technical transitions discussed in Geel, above n. 186.

196 See above n. 171.

197 Environmental Protection Agency, Carbon Pollution Emission Guidelines for Existing Stationary Sources: Electric Utility Generating Units, 80 Fed. Reg. 64,662 (October 23, 2015). From the perspective of China, a change of development model greatly contributed to setting new priorities in international climate negotiations. See I. Hilton, O. Kerr, 'The Paris Agreement: China's "New Normal" Role in International Climate Negotiations' (2017) 17 *Climate Policy* 48.

198 Clean Air Act, 42 U.S.C. §7401 et seq. (1970).

of the CAA to include carbon dioxide among air pollutants,[199] this delegation made legally possible the adoption of the CPP. What to a non-lawyer may look like a hardly noticeable difference in legal form is, in practice, very important for the prospects of the CPP and, accordingly, for those of the meaningful participation of the US in the Paris Agreement. This became manifest when in early February 2016 the US Supreme Court suspended the implementation of the CPP following legal action from a group of affected federated States and companies.[200] The challenge of the CPP provides a textbook illustration of how the stakeholders that are more involved in the current socio-technical regime and that, as a result, would lose more from a regime change can use legal means to hinder a sustainability transition or, at least, to gain time. That threat became more realistic after the election to the Presidency, in late 2016, of climate-sceptic Republican candidate. But the prospects for such an outcome had been foreseen by the previous administration and the text of the Paris Agreement itself was legally engineered to make it more difficult to repeal or defeat. Addressing the technicalities of this approach is less important here[201] than the broader point that the legal form of the transitional process is not without significant and potentially major consequences.

A similar analysis can be conducted in connection with the resilience of the energy transition policies (e.g. feed-in-tariff schemes) adopted by countries around the world, from Canada, to Spain, the Czech Republic or India, when assessed from the standpoint of international trade and investment law. Such policies are key to send a signal to the private sector to invest resources in the development and diffusion of technologies (from renewable energy equipment or generation to electric vehicles or efficient batteries). Law can create new markets and opportunities, and thereby it can promote a technological transition.[202] However, depending on the specific legal form of an energy policy intervention (e.g. whether the instrument has been adopted following due process standards, or is more or less proportional, or whether it subjects foreign and domestic producers and investors to different treatment), its legal resilience will not be the same, because it may be challenged before an international trade or investment tribunal.[203] Yet, it is sometimes the case, as for

199 *Massachusetts v. EPA* 549 U.S. 497 (2007).

200 Order in pending case, *West Virginia et al. v. EPA et al.* (February 9, 2016), 577 U.S.

201 See D. Wirth, 'Cracking the American Climate Negotiators' Hidden Code: United States Law and the Paris Agreement' (2016) 6 *Climate Law* 152.

202 See e.g. Jorge E. Viñuales, *Green Industrial Policy and Trade: A Tool-Box* (Geneva: PAGE, 2017).

203 See Jorge E. Viñuales, *Foreign Investment and the Environment in International Law* (Cambridge University Press, 2012, reprint 2015).

the CPP, that the features challenged are precisely the legal enablers necessary to make the adoption of the instrument politically possible.

A good illustration is provided by the subsidies scheme introduced by India to support local producers of renewable energy (solar) equipment. To understand the deeper implications of this case, it is useful to recall some conclusions of the literature on socio-technical transitions discussed earlier. One important aspect was the 'first in, last out; last in, first out' insight. Applied to China, South Korea, India and other emerging economies, this means that the cost of moving away from a given socio-technical regime and into a new one is lower for such countries, because they are less tied to the previous regime. In fact, embracing the new technology may provide a competitive advantage if and when the new socio-technical regime (based on a low-carbon energy matrix) becomes dominant. From a political perspective, it is then reasonable to expect that India will move in the direction of the new socio-technical regime not only because there are global benefits relating to climate change mitigation but also because, by doing so, it may give its industry an opportunity to position itself in the emerging socio-technical regime. This is precisely what the Indian renewable energy support scheme (India Solar Mission) tried to achieve by including local content ('buy local') requirements. In order to participate in the government electricity purchase programme introduced by India, a producer of electricity from renewable sources had to source its equipment from Indian producers. Such a measure is normally illegal under both international trade and investment disciplines and, following legal action from the US and others, a trade panel constituted under the aegis of the WTO found India in breach of its international trade obligations.[204]

Underlying this ruling – and the trade rules on which it is based – is the idea that trade must be liberalised to promote efficiency based on comparative advantage reasoning. If a foreign producer of solar energy equipment abroad is more efficient (it produces and sells at a lower price) than an Indian one, then its advantage must not be neutralised by governmental interference (protectionism). However, the operation of the rules can also be assessed in a different light. The overall operation of trade rules could be seen as a hindrance to an energy transition in one of the two most populated countries of the world. To the extent that for a country such as India it is not realistic to move massively into renewable energy if that amounts to subsidise foreign producers of renewable energy equipment, rather than local ones, then the question is whether we are serious in our constant efforts (including complex and costly

204 *India – Certain Measures Relating to Solar Cells and Solar Modules, Report of the Panel*, 24 April 2016, WT/DS456/R.

climate change negotiations) to push emerging economies into a low carbon energy matrix. It may be theoretically possible to ask such countries to both move into renewables and buy foreign products, as trade law seems to require, but it is hardly realistic and, even if they could be nudged in that direction, it is not necessarily fair. It may be useful to recall here the discussion earlier in this essay regarding global exchange systems, and the protectionist position taken by developed countries at the stage when they were developing new industries and technologies. Irrespective of the policy (and political) stance one may take on this question, the relevance of law and legal form in promoting or hindering sustainability transitions can hardly be questioned. As for the deeper normative question of the values that should be advanced by legal frameworks, this is also an area where law can play a key role.

3.4 Legitimising the Transition

A different conception of law underpins discussions of its role in providing legitimacy. I should begin by clarifying how I see the role of law as a legitimacy provider in this context. First, law can provide legitimacy by fleshing out certain policy interventions in such a way as to achieve a better result defined by reference to some pre-set goals (results-based legitimacy). Such is the case of the regulative conception of law as a pure technology, discussed earlier. The higher legitimacy of law comes in this case from the fact that it is better designed to achieve certain goals arising from a prior value choice. This is not what I have in mind here. Instead, I would like to discuss the role of law in legitimising the transition from two other perspectives. In one of these perspectives, law provides legitimacy because it enshrines certain pre-selected legal values. The difference with the previous approach is that the legitimacy provided by law rests on the sole consecration of the value and not in the capacity of law to optimise it. It is a deontological rather than a consequentialist logic. In the third perspective, law provides legitimacy not because it enshrines the values to be protected but because it organises a process that is expected to lead to the consecration of such end-values. To some extent, this perspective can be seen as a use of the first perspective to reach the second one. What is designed here is an appropriate process capable of leading to foundational – non-instrumental – values while respecting certain others – instrumental values. The latter point is important. Indeed, the design of the process parameters is not value-free. It rests on certain values (of what a proper process is expected to be) but such values are instrumental, their enshrinement in law is valued by reference to the ability to lead to the consecration of other – non-instrumental – values envisioned in the second perspective. I would like to illustrate how the second and third perspectives could illuminate the role of law in legitimising sustainability transitions.

From the *second perspective*, a fundamental legitimising role played by law is to translate into a consecrated or instituted form (even when such institution consists of an understanding of what customary or 'common' law is) some foundational values of a community, particularly certain rights and guarantees enshrined in a constitution. Much like the standard ethical systems discussed by Hans Jonas,[205] modern constitutional systems are broadly based on a human anthropology and an understanding of human agency that is challenged by the Anthropocene narrative. The modern conceptions of liberty and equality and the articulation between these two fundamental values are based on a culture of 'individualism', 'dignity' and 'progress', understood as the human ability to increasingly push back natural constraints, as well as of emancipation through freedom from nature and prosperity (development and growth) with no lasting impact on nature. Several significant contributions have been made to highlight the anthropocentric underpinnings of modern constitutions as well as to reformulate constitutionalism from an environmental perspective.[206] In an important contribution, Louis Kotzé has investigated the implications of the Anthropocene narrative for the understanding of constitutional law in a comparative and international perspective.[207] Relying on previous work on environmental constitutionalism, he explains that constitutional intervention

205 See above n. 57.

206 See particularly, in the German constitutional scholarship, the works of R. Steinberg, *Der ökologische Verfassungsstaat* (Frankfurt am Main: Suhrkamp, 1988) (relying on the earlier work of M. Kloepfer, who saw the environment as an intrinsic element for the existence of the State, now reinterpreted as 'Umweltstaat', Steinberg argues for an 'ecological constitutional State' in which protection of the environment is both instrumental (anthropocentric) and an end in itself); K. Bosselmann, *Im Namen der Natur: Der Weg zum ökologischen Rechtsstaat* (Bern: Scherz, 1992) (introducing the conception of an ecological rule of law, which seeks to depart from the overwhelmingly human-centred conception of modern constitutions, with its focus on human development as pushing the limits of – indeed, destroying – nature). In North-American constitutional scholarship the contributions follow a more empirical and comparative approach (see e.g. D. R. Boyd, *The Environmental Rights Revolution: A Global Study of Constitutions, Human Rights, and the Environment* (Vancouver: UBC Press, 2012) and J. R. May, E. Daly, *Global Environmental Constitutionalism* (Cambridge University Press, 2014)) although there have been major contributions to the reformulation of foundational legal categories (a classic example is C. Stone, 'Should Trees have Standing? Towards Legal Rights for Natural Objects' (1972) 45 *California Law Review* 450). Louis Kotzé provides a lucid account of these and other contributions in Kotzé, above n. 14, at 136–151.

207 Kotzé, above n. 14.

for environmental protection is the most effective – because the most fundamental – form of legal intervention. At the constitutional level, the relations between humans and nature can be genuinely redefined from a normative perspective, much in the same way as – in his experience as a South African – constitutional law has been able to structure South Africa's transition out the apartheid regime. He then reviews different ways in which the main dimensions of constitutionalism, including the rule of law, separation of powers, judicial review, constitutional supremacy, democratic rule and constitutional rights, could be revisited from an environmental protection perspective. Despite the significant effort displayed in this account, its fundamental premise seems to remain that an environmental reformulation of constitutional law, and its possible generalisation at the international level, are the best legal means to rise to the unprecedented challenge posed by the Anthropocene. As noted by Kotzé:

> The central hypothesis of this book is that 'ordinary' non-constitutional law, while crucial to mediating the human-environment interface, will not be sufficient to do so on its own in the Anthropocene. A form of constitutional law, most clearly explicated by environmental constitutionalism, is required to confront Anthropocene exigencies because of the social, political, juridical and regulatory advantages that constitutionalism holds out over 'ordinary' non-constitutional law.[208]

If this proposition means that 'environmental law' alone or, more specifically, 'ordinary' environmental law will not be sufficient to rise to the challenge, one can only agree. But I am less certain that an environmental re-interpretation or even re-design of constitutional law is the most far-reaching step that can be made from a legal perspective.

As I have endeavoured to show throughout this essay, there are myriad ways in which law has over the last two centuries prompted and sustained the advent of the Anthropocene, and they may all be engaged in attempting to manage the new proposed geological epoch. Changing the top of the pyramid would certainly be a major step. But what exactly is to be considered the top of the normative pyramid? Is it the constitution, understood from a top-down hierarchical perspective of law? Is it the bottom-up law of an inverted pyramid that governs commercial transactions, payments, property, labour, business organisation, and many other areas of human activity? Is it the international legal frameworks organising broad international flows of goods, services, capitals,

208 *Ibid.*, at 177.

people, waste, resources, knowledge or culture? Is it the very legal concepts pervading European-rooted legal discourse, whether constitutional or other, which carry a dominating and unsustainable ontology of human relations to nature? Is it all of this as well as the other ways in which law influences human behaviour at once? My view is that, at least from a methodological perspective, we must take the time to revisit all these different dimensions and understand their role in prompting and sustaining the Anthropocene. That is, I believe, a necessary first step. But the more we include, the higher the need for a meaningfully structured inquiry identifying a limited set of questions that relate to the inquiries conducted in other disciplines, whether in the humanities, social or natural sciences.

Constitutions may be, however, strategically important from the *third perspective* identified earlier, namely for the organisation of the processes through which value choices are enshrined into law, whether to amend the constitution or to reorganise labour or corporate law or even to create new subjects of law or redefine liability and causality. Thus, whatever the real location of the top of the pyramid – to continue with the observation made in the previous paragraph – law can provide legitimacy to the evolving value choices made and enshrined into law by organising processes that guide and regulate such choice processes. In political philosophy, this approach is commonly known as 'procedural justice',[209] whereby the value of the outcome comes from the process that is followed to reach it or, more specifically, from the respect of instrumental values underpinning the organisation of that very process. As an illustration of how law could provide legitimacy in such a context one could refer to the 'organic' part of most constitutions (which defines how the community is organised, the institutions and their powers and inter-relations) and, more specifically, to the rise in the last two decades of so-called procedural environmental rights granting individuals enhanced control powers over the environmental implications of production and consumption process: powers to know and to act directly (right of access to environmental information, right of participation in environmental decision-making, and access to justice).[210] This is, in my view, a strategically important way in which law can provide legitimacy to the choices driving a transition to sustainability: by organising processes – based on instrument values (organic parts in

209 For a foundational discussion see J. Rawls, *A Theory of Justice* (Cambridge MA: Harvard University Press, 1971, revised in 1999), section 14.

210 On this rise see J. Ebbesson, 'Principle 10: Public Participation', in J. E. Viñuales (ed.), *The Rio Declaration on Environment and Development. A Commentary* (Oxford University Press, 2015), at 287–310.

constitutions based on direct, semi-direct or representative democratic institutions or on a triad of environmental procedural rights) – that can lead to foundational societal choices.

Conclusion: A Research Agenda

The purpose of this last section is to pull all the threads unwound in the previous pages in order to provide a concise and hopefully meaningful agenda to guide legal research on the different dimensions of the Anthropocene. Importantly, the proposed agenda must be capable of integrating legal inquiry into the broader interdisciplinary efforts aimed at understanding the Anthropocene. For this reason, each of the three previous sections started with a detour or, in other words, a reference to the wider debate in the humanities, social and natural sciences, which provide both the foundations and the connection with the legal research agenda developed here. Within these broader questions, the proposed agenda must identify questions that are apposite for legal inquiry, i.e. questions for which legal inquiry is capable of providing relevant answers that cannot be provided by other disciplines. Finally, the agenda must both select an appropriate set of legal questions of sufficient generality and organise them into an overall coherent framework.

Based on these considerations, I would like to offer the following research agenda aimed at understanding the role of law in prompting, sustaining and potentially managing the Anthropocene:

1 *Ontological Dualism*

1.1 Broader Inquiry

The Anthropocene narrative challenges the widely held assumption that human progress consisted of pushing natural frontiers and constraints, within a natural theatre deemed to be immutable in a human timeframe. Such frontiers were seen as less and less relevant to the understanding of human activity as science and technology – hence human powers over nature – progressed. Instead, the Anthropocene narrative suggests that human and natural histories are intertwined, even within a short – human – timeframe, because what was believed to be progress with no adverse impact on the ability of the Earth system to regenerate is in fact modifying major geological cycles to such an extent that humans are a geological force whose impact on the Earth will be felt both in natural cycles and by humans themselves.

1.2 Within this broader inquiry a cluster of legal questions can be identified regarding:

i) The extent to which and the processes whereby law and legal concepts have been detached from nature, and the implications for the advent, sustaining and potential management of the Anthropocene;
ii) The extent to which law and legal concepts can express the unprecedented level of responsibility of humans as a geological force driving the Anthropocene;
iii) The extent to which legal orders can be adjusted through additional layers of norms – such as environmental law – or, instead, require a deeper reformulation of foundational concepts, with the ensuing imbrications of such reformulations, to address the challenges of the Anthropocene.

2 *Inequalities*

2.1 Broader Inquiry

Stating that 'humans' are the geological force behind the Anthropocene conceals profound intra-species inequalities between regions and groups of people in prompting, sustaining or suffering from the unsettling of natural cycles unveiled by the Anthropocene narrative. Understanding such inequalities is important both for allocating responsibilities and for addressing the social dynamics that prompted and sustained the Anthropocene and that will in all likelihood affect some groups more than others.

2.2 Within this broader inquiry a cluster of legal questions can be identified regarding:

i) The relation between a certain legal organisation of production – including the law governing business organisation, labour relations, and effects on third parties – and the inequalities underpinning the Anthropocene;
ii) The relation between the law governing exchange systems at the internal (including imperial) or international (bilateral, regional, global) levels and the processes prompting and sustaining the Anthropocene;
iii) How law can be used to allocate responsibilities for the past, present and future adverse impacts unveiled by the Anthropocene narrative among past, present and future groups of people.

3 *Transitions*

3.1 Broader Inquiry

Given the role of energy, transportation, agriculture and other foundational activities in prompting and sustaining the Anthropocene, it is necessary to understand the dynamics of transitions to other socio-technical regimes, including the emergence of pioneering technologies, the necessary period for their refinement and diffusion, the strong resistance from prior entrenched interests and, more generally, the many trade-offs entailed by the transition.

3.2 Within this broader inquiry a cluster of legal questions can be identified regarding:

i) The avenues to improve law and regulation as a technology to address the challenges of the Anthropocene;
ii) The ways in which law can promote or, conversely, hinder attempts to transition from one unsustainable socio-technical regime to a sustainable one;
iii) The legal ways of reflecting value choices or of organising processes to legitimise the choices entailed by such a transition.

Select Bibliography

Books and Edited Volumes

Anghie, A., *Imperialism, Sovereignty and the Making of International Law* (Cambridge University Press, 2004).

Armitage, D., *The Ideological Origins of the British Empire* (Cambridge University Press, 2000).

Austin, J., *The Province of Jurisprudence Determined* (London: John Murray, 1832).

Bentham, J., *Of Laws in General* (London: Athlone Press, 1970 [1782]).

Berkes, F., J. Folke, C. Colding (eds.), *Navigating Social-Ecological Systems. Building Resilience for Complexity and Change* (Cambridge University Press, 2003).

Berle, A., G. Means, *The Modern Corporation and Private Property* (New York: Macmillan, 1932).

Bonneuil, C., J.-B. Fressoz, *L'événement Anthropocène. La Terre, l'histoire et nous* (Paris: Seuil, 2016).

Bosselmann, K., *Im Namen der Natur: Der Weg zum ökologischen Rechtsstaat* (Bern: Scherz, 1992).

Boyd, D. R., *The Environmental Rights Revolution: A Global Study of Constitutions, Human Rights, and the Environment* (Vancouver: UBC Press, 2012).

Brown Weiss, E., *In Fairness to Future Generations: International Law, Common Patrimony and Intergenerational Equity* (United Nations University, 1989).

Cottrel, P. L., *Industrial Finance 1830–1914. The finance and organization of the English manufacturing industry* (London: Routledge, 1980).

Croce, B., *La filosofia di Giambattista Vico* (Bari: Laterza, 2nd edn 1922).

Davies, A. C. L., *Perspectives on Labour Law* (Cambridge University Press, 2nd edn. 2009).

De Greif, P. (ed.), *The Handbook of Reparations* (Oxford University Press, 2008).

Dworkin, R., *Justice in Robes* (Cambridge MA: Harvard University Press, 2006).

Dupuy, P.-M, J. E. Viñuales, *International Environmental Law* (Cambridge University Press, 2015, 2nd edn. 2018).

Elster, J., *Closing the Books: Transition Justice in Historical Perspective* (Cambridge University Press, 2004).

Fast, J., *Beyond Bullying: Breaking the Cycle of Shame, Bullying and Violence* (Oxford University Press, 2016).

Fischer-Kowalski, M., H. Haberl (eds.), *Socioecological Transitions and Global Change: Trajectories of Social Metabolism and Land Use* (Cheltenham: Edward Elgar, 2007).

Forbath, W. E., *Law and the Shaping of the American Labor Movement* (Cambridge, Mass.: Harvard University Press, 1991).

Foster, J. B., B. Clark, R. York, *The Ecological Rift. Capitalism War on the Earth* (Monthly Review Press, 2010).

Freestone, D., C. Streck (eds.), *Legal Aspects of Carbon Trading* (Oxford University Press, 2009).

Garmestani, A. S., C. R. Allen (eds.), *Social–Ecological Resilience and Law* (New York: Columbia University Press, 2014).

Glaser, B., G. Krause, B. M. W. Ratter, M. Welp (eds.), *Human-Nature Interactions in the Anthropocene* (London: Routledge, 2012).

Georgescu-Roegen, N., *The Enthropy Law and the Economic Process* (Cambridge MA: Harvard University Press, 1971).

Grinlinton, D., P. Taylor (eds), *Property Rights and Sustainability: The Evolution of Property Rights to meet Ecological Challenges* (Leiden: Martinus Nijhoff, 2011).

Hamilton, C., F. Gemenne, C. Bonneil (eds.), *The Anthropocene and the Global Environmental Crisis: Rethinking Modernity in a New Epoch* (London: Routledge, 2015).

Hart, H. L. A., *The Concept of Law* (Oxford: Clarendon Press, 1961).

Hinteregger, M. (ed.), *Environmental Liability and Ecological Damage in European Law* (Cambridge University Press, 2008).

Holtzmann, H., E. Kristjánsdóttir (eds.), *International Mass Claims Processes* (Oxford University Press, 2007).

Hornborg, H., *Global Ecology and Unequal Exchange. Fetishism in a Zero-Sum World* (London: Routledge, 2013).

Hornborg, H., C. L. Crumley (ed.), *The World System and the Earth System* (Walnut Creek CA: Left Coast Press, 2006).

Jonas, H., *Das Prinzip Verantwortung. Versuch einer Ethik für die technologische Zivilisation* (Frankfurt am Main: Suhrkamp, 1979).

Kahn-Freund, O., *Labour Relations: Heritage and Adjustment* (Oxford University Press, 1979).

Kander, A. et al., *Power to the People. Energy in Europe over the Last Five Centuries* (Princeton NJ: Princeton University Press, 2012).

Kelsen, H., *Reine Rechtslehre: Einleitung in die rechtswissenschaftiche Problematik* (Leipzig; Wien: F. Deuticke, 1934).

Kelsen, H., *General Theory of Law and the State* (Cambridge MA: Harvard University Press, 1945).

Kotzè, L., *Global Environmental Constitutionalism in the Anthropocene* (Oxford: Hart Publishing, 2016).

Landes, D. S., *The Unbound Prometheus. Technological Change and Industrial Development in Western Europe from 1750 to the Present* (Cambridge University Press, 2nd edn 2003).

Lazarus, R., *The Making of Environmental Law* (Chicago IL: University of Chicago Press, 2004).

Lees, E., J. E. Vinuales (eds), *The Oxford Handbook of Comparative Environmental Law* (Oxford University Press, forthcoming 2018).

Le Goff, J., *Du silence à la parole. Une histoire du droit du travail des années 1830 à nos jours* (Rennes: Presses universitaires de Rennes, 2004).

Linder, M., *The Employment Relationship in Anglo-American Law: A Historical Perspective* (New York: Greenwood, 1989).

Loening, T. C., *The Reconciliation Agreement of 403/402 B.C. in Athens* (Stuttgard: Franz Steiner Verlag, 1987).

Lorius, C., L. Carpentier, *Voyage dans l'Anthropocène: cette nouvelle ère dont nous sommes les héros* (Arles: Actes Sud, 2010).

Malm, A., *Fossil Capital. The Rise of Steam-Power and the Roots of Global Warming* (London: Verso, 2016).

Massard-Guilbaud, G., *Histoire de la pollution industrielle en France, 1789–1914* (Paris: EHESS, 2010).

May, J. R., E. Daly, *Global Environmental Constitutionalism* (Cambridge University Press, 2014).

Moore, J. W., *Capitalism in the Web of Life* (London: Verso, 2015).

Nesbit, M., A. Illés, *Establishing an EU 'Guardian for Future Generations', Report and recommendations for the World Future Council* (London: Institute for European Environmental Policy, 2015).

Nicholls, A. (ed.), *Social Entrepreneurship. New Models of Sustainable Social Change* (Oxford University Press, 2006).
Pomeranz, K., *The Great Divergence: China, Europe and the Making of the Modern World Economy* (Princeton NJ: Princeton University Press, 2000).
Putnam, P. C., *Energy in the Future* (New York: Van Nostrand, 1953).
Rawls, J., *A Theory of Justice* (Cambridge MA: Harvard University Press, 1971, revised in 1999).
Reid, A., *United We Stand. A History of Britain's Trade Unions* (London: Penguin, 2005).
Rossi, P., *I segni del tempo: storia della Terra e storia delle nazioni da Hooke a Vico* (Milano: Feltrinelli, 1979).
Roy, W. G., *Socialising Capital: The Rise of the Large Industrial Corporation in America* (Princeton NJ: Princeton University Press, 1997).
Russell, E., *Evolutionary History: Uniting History and Biology to Understand Life on Earth* (Cambridge University Press, 2011).
Schurr, S. H., B. C. Netschert, *Energy in the American Economy 1850–1975* (Baltimore: John Hopkins Press, 1960).
Schonhardt-Bailey, C. (ed.), *The Rise of Free Trade* (London: Routledge, 1997).
Schonhardt-Bailey, C., *From the Corn Laws to Free Trade: Interests, Ideas and Institutions in Historical Perspective* (Cambridge MA: MIT Press, 2006).
Seavoy, R. E., *The origins of the American business corporation 1784–1855* (Westport, Conn.: Greenwood Press, 1982).
Shrijver, N., *Sovereignty over Natural Resources. Balancing Rights and Duties* (Cambridge University Press, 1997).
Smail, D. L., *On Deep History and the Brain* (Berkeley: University of California Press, 2008).
Smil, V., *Energy in World History* (Boulder CO: Westview Press, 1994).
Supiot, A., *Critique du droit du* travail (Paris: Presses universitaires de France, 2007).
Steinberg, R., *Der ökologische Verfassungsstaat* (Frankfurt am Main: Suhrkamp, 1988).
Thomas, H., *The Slave Trade: The Story of the Atlantic Slave Trade, 1440–1870* (New York: Simon & Schuster, 1997).
UN Secretary-General, *Intergenerational Solidarity and the Needs of Future Generations. Report of the Secretary-General*, 15 August 2013, UN Doc A/68/322.
van Zeben, J., *The Allocation of Regulatory Competence in the EU Emissions Trading Scheme* (Cambridge University Press, 2014).
Viñuales, J. E., *Foreign Investment and the Environment in International Law* (Cambridge University Press, 2012, reprint 2015).
Viñuales, J. E. (ed.), *The Rio Declaration on Environment and Development. A Commentary* (Oxford University Press, 2015).
Viñuales, J. E., *Green Industrial Policy and Trade: A Tool-Box* (Geneva: PAGE, 2017).

Wallerstein, I., *World System Analysis: An Introduction* (Durham NC: Duke University Press, 2004).

Wallerstein, I., *The Modern World-System, vol. I: Capitalist Agriculture and the Origins of the European World-Economy in the Sixteenth Century* (New York/London: Academic Press, 1974).

Wallerstein, I., *The Modern World-System, vol. II: Mercantilism and the Consolidation of the European World-Economy, 1600–1750* (New York/London: Academic Press, 1980).

Wallerstein, I., *The Modern World-System, vol. III: The Second Great Expansion of the Capitalist World-Economy, 1730–1840's* (San Diego: Academic Press, 1989).

Weber, M., *Wirtschaft und Gesellschaft. Grundriss der verstehenden Soziologie* (Tubingen: J. C. B. Mohr, 4th edn 1956).

Wilson, C., *Meta-analysis of Unit and Industry Level Scaling Dynamics in Energy Technologies and Climate Change Mitigation Scenarios*, IR-09-029 (Laxenburg: International Institute for Applied Systems Analysis, 2009).

Whitehead, M., *Environmental Transformations: A Geography of the Anthropocene* (New York: Routledge, 2014).

Yearbook of International Environmental Law (2014) 25 (1).

Yunus, M., K. Weber, *Building Social Business* (New York: Public Affairs, 2010).

Articles and Chapters in Edited Volumes

Ambrusné, E. T., 'The Parliamentary Commissioner for Future Generations of Hungary and his impact' (2010) 10/1 *Intergenerational Justice Review* 18.

Bairoch, P., 'European trade policy, 1815–1914', in P. Mathias and S. Pollard (eds), *The Cambridge Economic* History *of Europe* (Cambridge University Press, 1989), vol. 8, pp. 1–160.

Baker, S. H., 'Adaptive Law in the Anthropocene' (2015) 90 *Chicago-Kent Law Review* 563.

Bennet, E. M., S. R. Carpenter, N. F. Caraco, 'Human Impact on Erodable Phosphorus and Eutrophication: A Global Perspective' (2001) 51/3 *BioScience* 227.

Bennett, E., G. D. Peterson, L. J. Gordon, 'Understanding relationships among multiple ecosystem services' (2009) 12/12 *Ecology Letters* 1394.

Benvenisti, E., 'Sovereigns as Trustees of Humanity: On the Acocuntability of States to Foreign Stateholders (2013) 107/2 *American Journal of International Law* 295.

Biber, E., 'Law in the Anthropocene Epoch' (2016) *UC Berkeley Public Law Research Paper No. 2834037*.

Biermann, F. et al., 'Down to Earth: Contextualizing the Anthropocene' (2016) 39 *Global Environmental Change* 341.

Blair, M. M., 'Locking in Capital: What Corporate Law Achieved for Business Organizers in the Nineteenth Century' (2003) 51 *UCLA Law Review* 387.

Brenner, J. F., 'Nuisance Law and the Industrial Revolution' (1974) 3/2 *Journal of Legal Studies* 403.

Brondizio, E. et al., 'Re-conceptualizing the Anthropocene: A call for collaboration' (2016) 39 *Global Environmental Change* 318.

Bosselmann, K., K. Rakhyun and K. Bosselmann, 'International Environmental Law in the Anthropocene: Towards a Purposive System of Multilateral Environmental Agreements' (2013) 2 *Transnational Environmental Law* 285.

Brown Weiss, E., 'The Planetary Trust: Conservation and Intergenerational Equity', (1984) 11 *Ecology Law Quarterly* 495.

Carroll, A. B., 'A History of Corporate Social Responsibility: Concepts and Practices', in A. Crane et al. (eds.), *The Oxford Handbook of Corporate Social Responsibility* (Oxford University Press, 2008), pp. 19–45.

Castree, N. et al., 'Changing the intellectual climate' (2014) 4 *Nature Climate Change* 763.

Castree, N., 'The Anthropocene and the Environmental Humanities: Extending the Conversation' (2014) 5 *Environmental Humanities* 233.

Chakrabarty, D., 'The climate of history: four theses' (2009) 35 *Critical Inquiry* 197.

Chase, K. A., 'Imperial protection and strategic trade policy in the interwar period' (2004) 11/1 *Review of International Political Economy* 177.

Cohen, D., 'The rhetoric of justice: strategies of reconciliation and revenge in the restoration of Athenian democracy in 403 BC' (2001) 42/2 *Archives européennes de sociologie* 335.

Costanza, R., 'What is Ecological Economics?' (1989) 1 *Ecological Economics* 1.

Crutzen, P. J., E. Stoermer, *'The «Anthropocene»'* (2000) 41 *IGBP Global Change Newsletter* 17.

Crutzen, P. J., 'Geology of Mankind' (2002) 415 *Nature* 23.

Cullet, P., 'Principle 7: Common but Differentiated Responsibilities', in J. E. Viñuales (ed.), *The Rio Declaration on Environment and Development. A Commentary* (Oxford University Press, 2015), pp. 229–244.

Diaz, R. J., R. Rosenberg, 'Spreading dead zones and consequences for marine ecosystems' (2008) 321/5891 *Science* 926.

Dingle, A. E., 'The Monster Nuisance of All. Landowners, Alkali Manufacturers, and Air Pollution, 1828–1864' (1982) 35/4 *Economic History Review* 529.

Ebbesson, J., 'Principle 10: Public Participation', in J. E. Viñuales (ed.), *The Rio Declaration on Environment and Development. A Commentary* (Oxford University Press, 2015), pp. 287–310.

Ellis, E. C., 'Anthropogenic transformation of the terrestrial biosphere' (2011) 369/1938 *Philosophical Transactions of the Royal Society* 1010.

Emerich, Y., 'Regard civiliste sur le droit des biens de la common law: pour une conception transsystémique de la propriété' (2008) 38 *Revue générale de droit* 339.

Foster, J. B., B. Clark, 'Ecological imperialism and the global metabolic rift: Unequal exchange and the guano/nitrates trade' (2009) 50 *International Journal of Comparative Sociology* 311.

Foster, J. B., H. Holleman, 'The theory of unequal ecological exchange: A Marx-Odum dialectic' (2014) 41 *Journal of Peasant Studies* 199.

Fouquet, R., P. J. G. Pearson, 'A thousand years of energy use in the United Kingdom' (1998) 19/4 *The Energy Journal* 1.

Francioni, F., 'Realism, Utopia and the Future of International Environmental Law', in A. Cassese (ed.), *Realizing Utopia. The Future of International Law* (Oxford University Press, 2012), pp. 442–460.

Frankel, M., 'Obsolescence and technological change in a maturing economy' (1955) 45(3) *American Economic Review* 296.

Freedeman, C. E., *Joint-stock enterprise in France, 1807–1867: From privileged company to modern corporation* (Chapel Hill: University of North Carolina Press, 1970).

Fressoz, J.-B., 'Payer pour polluer: l'industrie chimique et la compensation des dommages environnementaux, 1800–1850' (2013) 28/1 *Histoire & mesure* 145.

Gales, B. et al., 'North versus south: energy transitions and energy intensity in Europe over 200 years' (2006) 11/2 *European Review of Economic History* 219.

Galloway, J. N. et al., 'Transformation of the nitrogen cycle: recent trends, questions, and potential solutions' (2008) 320/5879 *Science* 889.

Geels, F., 'The multi-level perspective in sustainability transitions: Response to seven criticisms' (2011) 1 *Environmental Innovation and Societal Transitions* 24.

Guinnane, T. W. et al., 'Pouvoir et proprieté dans l'entreprise : Pour une histoire international des sociétés à responsabilité limitée' (2008) 63/1 *Annales. Histoire. Sciences Sociales* 73.

Grinevald, J., 'L'effet de serre et la civilisation thermo-industrielle 1896–1996' (1997) 108 *Revue européenne des sciences sociales* 141.

Grubler, A., 'Time for a change: On the patterns of diffusion of innovation' (1996) 125/3 *Daedalus* 19.

Grubler, A., 'Energy transitions research: Insights and cautionary tales' (2012) 50 *Energy Policy* 8.

Hansmann, H., R. Kraakman, R. Squire, 'Law and the Rise of the Firm' (2005/2006) 119 *Harvard Law Review* 1335.

Hébié, M., 'Principle 6: Special Situation of Developing Countries', in J. E. Viñuales (ed.), *The Rio Declaration on Environment and Development. A Commentary* (Oxford University Press, 2015), pp. 207–228.

Hilton, I., O. Kerr, 'The Paris Agreement: China's 'New Normal' Role in International Climate Negotiations' (2017) 17 *Climate Policy* 48.

Honoré, A. M., 'Ownership', in A. G. Guest (ed.), *Oxford Essays in Jurisprudence* (Oxford University Press, 1961), pp. 107–147.

Horn, N., 'Aktienrechtliche Unternehmensorganisation in der Hochindustrialisierung (1860–1920)', in N. Horn, J. Kocka (eds.), *Recht und Entwicklung der Grossunternehmen im 19. und frühen 20. Jahrhundert: wirtschafts-, sozial- und rechtshistorische Untersuchungen zur Industrialisierung in Deutschland, Frankreich, England und den USA* (Göttingen: Vandenhoeck & Ruprecht, 1979), pp. 123–189.

Hornborg, A., 'Ecological economics, Marxism, and technological progress: Some explorations of the conceptual foundations of theories of ecological unequal exchange' (2014) 105 *Ecological Economics* 11.

Jonas, H., 'Philosophy at the End of the Century: Survey of its Past and Future' (1994) 61/4 *Social Research* 815.

Kahn-Freund, O., 'Legal Framework', in A. Flanders, H. A. Clegg (eds.), *The System of Industrial Relations in Great Britain: its History, Law and Institutions* (Oxford: Blackwell, 1954), pp. 42–127.

Kotzé, L., 'Rethinking Global Environmental Law and Governance in the Anthropocene' (2014) 32 *Journal of Energy and Natural Resources Law* 121.

Kotzé, L., 'Human Rights and the Environment in the Anthropocene' (2014) 1 *The Anthropocene Review* 1.

Lampe, M., 'Explaining nineteenth-century bilateralism: economic and political determinants of the Cobden–Chevalier network' (2011) 64/2 *Economic History Review* 644.

Laremont, R., 'Political versus Legal Strategies for the African Slavery Reparations Movement' (1999) 2/4 *African Studies Quarterly* 13.

Lewis, S. L., M. A. Maslin, 'Defining the Anthropocene' (2015) 519 *Nature* 171.

Li Q. Q. et al., 'Persistent organic pollutants and adverse health effects in humans' (2006) 69/21 *Journal of Toxicology and Environmental Health/A* 1987.

Malm, A. and A. Hornborg, 'The geology of mankind? A critique of the Anthropocene narrative' (2014) 1/1 *The Anthropocene Review* 62.

Mazrui, A., 'Global Africa: From Abolitionists to Reparationists' (1994) 37/3 *African Studies Review* 1.

Mazrui, A., 'From Slave Ship to Space Ship: Africa between Marginalization and Globalization' (1999) 2/4 *African Studies Quarterly* 5.

Mercure, J.-F. et al., 'Modelling complex systems of heterogeneous agents to better design sustainability transitions policy', (2016) 37 *Global Environmental Change* 102.

Molinari, C., 'Principle 3: From a Right to Development to Intergenerational Equity', in J. E. Viñuales (ed.), *The Rio Declaration on Environment and Development. A Commentary* (Oxford University Press, 2015), pp. 139–156.

O'Rourke, K. H., 'Tariffs and Growth in the Late 19th Century' (2000) 110 *The Economic Journal* 456.

Orr, J. C. et al., 'Anthropogenic ocean acidification over the twenty-first century and its impact on calcifying organisms' (2005) 437 *Nature* 681.

Palsson, G. et al., 'Reconceptualizing the 'Anthropos' in the Anthropocene: integrating the social sciences and humanities in global environmental change research' (2013) 28 *Environmental Science and Policy* 1.

Pimm, S. L. et al., 'The biodiversity of species and their rates of extinction, distribution, and protection' (2014) 344/6187 *Science* 987.

Pontin, B., 'Tort Law and Victorian Governement Growth: the historiographical significance of tort law in the shadow of chemical pollution' (1998) 18/4 *Oxford Journal of Legal Studies* 661.

Pope, J., 'Worker Lawmaking, Sit-Down Strikes, and the Shaping of American Industrial Relations, 1935–1958' (2006) 24/1 *Law & History Review* 45.

Pope, J., 'Contract, Race and Freedom of Labor in the Constitutional Law of 'Involuntary Servitude'' (2010) 119 *Yale Law Journal* 1474.

Priel, D., 'Toward Classical Legal Positivism' (2015) 101 *Virginia Law Review* 987.

Rajamani, L., 'Ambition and Differentiation in the 2015 Paris Agreement: Interpretative Possibilities and Underlying Politics' (2016) 65/2 *International and Comparative Law Quarterly* 493.

Robin, L., W. Steffen, 'History for the Anthropocene' (2007) 5/5 *History Compass* 1694.

Robinson, N., 'Beyond Sustainability: Environmental Management for the Anthropocene Epoch' (2012) 12 *Journal of Public Affairs* 181.

Robinson, N., 'Fundamental Principles of Law for the Anthropocene?' (2014) 44 *Environmental Policy and Law* 1.

Rockstrom, J. et al., 'A safe operating space for humanity' (2009) 461 *Nature* 472.

Sax, J. L., 'The Public Trust Doctrine in Natural Resources Law: Effective Judicial Intervention' (1970) 68 *Michigan Law Review* 471.

Schaffartzik, A. et al., 'The global metabolic transition: Regional patterns and trends of global material flows, 1950–2010' (2014) 26 *Global Environmental Change* 87.

Schandl, H., N. Schulz, 'Changes in the United Kingdom's natural relations in terms of society's metabolism and land-use from 1850 to the present day' (2002) 41 *Ecological Economics* 203.

Shoham, S., N. Lamay, 'Commission for future generations in the Knesset: Lessons learnt', in J. C. Tremmel (ed.), *Handbook of Intergenerational Justice* (Cheltenham: Edward Elgar, 2006), pp. 244–281.

Scott, K. N., 'International law in the Anthropocene: Responding to the Geoengineering Challenge' (2012) 34 *Michigan Journal of International Law* 309.

Smil, V., 'World History and Energy' (2004) *Encyclopedia of Energy* vol. 1, pp. 549–561.

Steffen, W., P. J. Crutzen, J. R. McNeil, 'The Anthropocene: Are humans now overwhelming the great forces of nature?' (2007) 36/8 *Ambio* 614.

Steffen, W., J. Grinevald, P. J. Crutzen, J. R. McNeill, 'The Anthropocene: Conceptual and historical perspectives' (2011) 369/1938 *Philosophical Transactions of the Royal Society* 842.

Stone, C., 'Should Trees have Standing? Towards Legal Rights for Natural Objects' (1972) 45 *California Law Review* 450.

Thomson, D., 'The Debt Has Not Been Paid, the Accounts Have Not Been Settled' (1999) 2/4 *African Studies Quarterly* 19.

Tremmel, J. C., 'Establishing intergenerational justice in national constitutions', in J. C. Tremmel (ed.), *Handbook of Intergenerational Justice* (Cheltenham: Edward Elgar, 2006), pp. 187–216.

Trubek, D. M., 'Max Weber on Law and the Rise of Capitalism' (1972) *Wisconsin Law Review* 720.

Vidas, D., O. K. Fauchald, Ø. Jensen, M. W. Tvedt, 'International law for the Anthropocene? Shifting perspectives in regulation of the oceans environment and genetic resources' (2015) 9 *Anthropocene* 1.

Viñuales, J. E., 'Balancing Effectiveness and Fairness in the Re-design of the Climate Change Regime' (2011) 24/1 *Leiden Journal of International Law* 223.

Walton, G. M., 'The New Economic History and the Burdens of the Navigation Acts' (1971) 24/4 *Economic History Review* 533.

Waters, C. N. et al. (2016) 'The Anthropocene is functionally and stratigraphically distinct from the Holocene' (2016) 351/6269 *Science* aad2622–1.

Williston, S., 'History of the Law of Business Corporations before 1800' (1888) 2/3–4 *Harvard Law Review* 105 (part 1), 149 (part 2).

Wirth, D., 'Cracking the American Climate Negotiators' Hidden Code: United States Law and the Paris Agreement' (2016) 6 *Climate Law* 152.

Zalasiewicz, J. et al., 'When did the Anthropocene begin? A mid-twentieth century boundary level is stratigraphically optimal' (2015) 383 *Quaternary international* 196.

www.ingramcontent.com/pod-product-compliance
Lightning Source LLC
Chambersburg PA
CBHW031332230926
51848CB00001B/207
9789004381353